W9-DIO-904

Free Prices Now!

Free Prices Now!

Fixing the Economy
by
Abolishing the Fed

Hunter Lewis

AC² Books
94 Landfill Road
Edinburg, VA 22824
888.542.9467   info@AC2Books.com

Free Prices Now!: Fixing the Economy by Abolishing the Fed © 2013 by AC²
Books. All rights reserved. Printed in the United States of America. No part
of this book may be used or reproduced in any manner whatsoever without written permission except in the case of brief quotations used in critical articles and reviews.

Publisher's Cataloging-in-Publication
(Provided by Quality Books, Inc.)

Lewis, Hunter.
        Free prices now! : fixing the economy by abolishing the Fed /
    Hunter Lewis.
        p. cm.
        Includes bibliographical references and index.
        LCCN 2013935436
        ISBN 978-0-9887267-0-3
        1. Price regulation--United States. 2. United States--Economic policy.
    3. United States--Economic conditions. I. Title.

    HB236.U5L49 2013
    338.5'26'0973

                                                    QBI13-600052

Contents

Part 4: Price Controllers and Crony Capitalists

Part 5: Reform

Part 1

1

Introduction

[Soviet] socialism collapsed because
it did not tell the economic truth.

—OYSTEIN DAHLE[1]

WHY IS THE human race so poor? Why do billions still lack enough even to eat?

As this author noted in an earlier book, even a small sum of money, such as $10, if compounded at 3% over 1,000 years, would produce a sum equal to twice the world's wealth today. It should be ridiculously easy, over time, to end human poverty. Why have we failed to do so?

Safety is certainly an important factor. No one will bring wealth out of hiding, much less invest it, if it is likely to be stolen. But protection from outright theft is not enough. We need an honest system of mutual exchange. A corrupt and dishonest economic system does not create wealth; it destroys it.

The most reliable barometer of economic honesty is to be found in prices. Honest prices, neither manipulated or controlled, provide both investors and consumers with reliable economic signals. They show, beyond any doubt, what is scarce, what is plentiful, where opportunities lie, and where they do not lie.

A corrupt economic system does not want honest prices, honest information, or honest results. The truth may be inconvenient or unprofitable for powerful government leaders or private interests allied with them. Typically, throughout human history, these leaders and special interests have sought to use their power to manipulate and control prices to their own advantage.

Much of the time, powerful price manipulators and controllers are accompanied and assisted by ideologists or theoreticians. These professional advisors—modern day Magi, skilled verbally or in mathematics—confidently argue that dishonest prices are really honest; honest prices are really dishonest; the resulting chaos is really order; and a future filled with jobs and plenty lies ahead with just a few more manipulations and controls. Sometimes the arguments are presented with calculated deceit, sometimes with muddled sincerity.

Can it really be this simple, that job growth and economic prosperity depend on allowing economic prices to tell the truth, free from the self-dealing and self-interested theories of powerful special interests? That is the central thesis of this book, and each chapter will explore it from an additional angle. What is needed to pull humanity out of dire poverty is a free price system, one that is neither manipulated nor controlled.

If prices are not free, an economic system cannot be expected to function properly. What happens thereafter will depend on the degree of price manipulation or control. If it is not extreme, the economy may limp along, impaired, not realizing its full potential, but not in overt crisis.

If the undermining of free prices is extreme enough, the system will visibly falter and may even collapse, as in 1929 or 2008. In this case, capital, jobs, and people's lives are destroyed. Ironically, the crisis often leads to a government response which entails even more price manipulation and control, and which therefore guarantees even more trouble, if not immediately, then down the road.

A further irony of all this is that a large majority of professional economists, including those aligned on the political "left" as well as "right," respond to surveys by indicating that they generally oppose "government price controls." The problem is that most government price manipulations and controls are not advertised as such. They may be stealthy by design, or they may just take a form that is not easily recognized for what it is.

Throughout this book, one of its aims will be to unmask these misguided government actions and show that they are indeed price manipulations and controls. We will also try to explain why they are doing untold damage to the hopes and prospects of anyone who depends on the economy, especially the poor.

Part 2

The Free Price System[*]

---

* This section covers material that will be familiar to readers of the author's *Are the Rich Necessary? Great Economic Arguments and How They Reflect Our Personal Values* (Mt. Jackson, VA: Axios Press, 2009). Those readers may wish to review Part Two briefly or proceed directly to Part Three.

2

Why We Need Free Prices

IMAGINE GETTING UP one morning and discovering that there are no longer any prices. What complete chaos there would be, chaos that would soon lead to shortages, starvation, and social collapse! Without any prices, we would be back to a barter system, and the world's present population could not even be fed, housed, or clothed by barter. Prices help us survive and thrive by enormously simplifying economic life. They do not tell us everything, but they tell us enough to make decisions.

Let's say that I am a tomato sauce producer. If the price of tomato sauce is higher than the price of the inputs (tomatoes, olive oil, spices, glass jars, labels, processing facilities, etc.), I will probably decide to make tomato sauce.

I do not know why these prices are what they are. Is it because demand is rising or falling? Or is it supply? I do not need to know in order to produce (or to consume). Prices lead me and other market participants to act in ways that balance demand and supply and, by doing so, to give people as much as possible of what they want.

What happens if the flow of information from prices is interrupted by government price manipulations or controls? If I am unaware of what is happening, I may make poor decisions. If I become aware of what is happening, I may become afraid to make any decisions at all. Either way my employees may lose their jobs or at least their raises.

During the 18th century, there were frequent bread shortages in France. This is when Queen Marie Antoinette is supposed to have exclaimed, when told that the peasants were starving from lack of bread, "Why, let them eat cake!" The French government was not much more sensible in dealing with the crisis. It placed price controls on bread, since scarcity was driving the price higher.

The intention was to make bread more affordable. The cost of growing wheat was also rising, however, so that the wheat farmers realized they would have to sell at a loss. Not surprisingly, they stopped planting, and the price of bread rose even higher.

Jacques Turgot, Controller-General of France, tried to introduce free price reforms. But government officials and allied business interests—crony capitalists, in today's terminology—quickly forced his resignation. This in turn sealed the fate of the regime, and eventually cost the monarch his life as well as that of his wife Marie Antoinette. In 1770, Turgot wrote that

> [The French monarchy] fanc[ied] that it
> ensured abundance of grain by making the
> condition of the cultivator more uncertain
> and unhappy than that of all other citizens.[2]

Governments have imposed outright price controls on goods for thousands of years. King Hammurabi literally carved prices in stone on a monument placed in ancient Babylon about four thousand years ago. As demand and supply shifted, one can only imagine the havoc caused by these legally mandated, never-changing prices.

The communist government that followed the Russian Revolution of 1917 faced a particularly troublesome decision about prices. Its leaders knew that they intended to abolish private property and private profits. In that case, what to do about prices? Should they be kept? It seemed unimaginable to abolish prices completely. But with private property and private property transactions outlawed, who would set prices and how would it be done?

This was complicated by a curious omission on Karl Marx's part. The founder of communism had never, in all three fat volumes of his work *Capital*, bothered to explain exactly how his version of socialism would work. There was no blueprint on which to draw nor even specific instructions about prices or profits.

Faced with this quandary, the Soviet planners decided that public officials would set prices and any profits would accrue to the state. British economist John Maynard Keynes praised these efforts:

> Let us not belittle these magnificent experiments or refuse to learn from them. . . . The Five Year Plan in Russia, the Corporative state [devised by Mussolini] in Italy; . . . and state planning [under] democracy in Great Britain. . . . Let us hope that they will all be successful. [3]

Economist Ludwig von Mises sharply disagreed with this. He argued in a 1920 article ("Economic Calculation in the Socialist Commonwealth") and a 1922 book (*Socialism)* that the Soviet system was unworkable. Prices set by government officials could not possibly provide the information needed to make efficient decisions about the allocation of capital and labor.

A flourishing modern economy requires billions of such decisions. How could government officials, however expert, know enough or learn enough to make sense of all the masses of price interrelationships or even be able to define them? Soviet planners developed equations that may have helped, but no equation could cope with the multidimensionality of an economy, something that private prices, directed by no one, manage with ease.

As von Mises said:

> It is not enough to tell a man not to buy on the cheapest market and not to sell on the dearest market. . . . One must establish unambiguous rules for the guidance of conduct in each concrete situation.[4]

Von Mises student Friedrich Hayek added that markets are a

discovery system.

They discover what is scarce, what is available. They communicate it through prices.

Communist and many other economists tried to prove von Mises and Hayek wrong, but never got very far. By 1960, the Soviet Union had five to nine price systems, according to different accounts, and probably did not actually know how many it had. None of them worked, despite the expedient of "borrowing" prices from market economies in the Europe and elsewhere.[5] This failure led directly to the fall of communism.

The fall of communism is not a reason for governments of so-called market economies to congratulate themselves. They may not attempt to control all prices, as the Soviet planners did. But they are not allowing prices to tell the economic truth either.

3

The Role of Profits in Driving Down Prices

PROFITS ARE AN integral part of any free price system. If people are free to set the prices for what they are selling, they will naturally try to set the price high enough to earn a profit. This actually works to everyone's, not just the seller's, advantage.

Some people believe that a profit margin (what the producer earns over and above cost) makes goods or services more expensive. Philosopher Ted Honderich expresses this viewpoint:

> If there are two ways of [producing] some valuable thing, and the second way involves not only the costs of [producing] it ... but

also [unnecessary] profits of millions or billions of dollars or pounds, then . . . the second way is patently and tremendously less efficient.[6]

Honderich could not be more wrong. Imagine that my tomato sauce business (Chapter 2) is earning a very fat profit. Most likely I will take those profits and use them to increase production. I will want to increase production in order to earn even more fat profits. Other tomato sauce producers will likely do the same, and some companies not presently making tomato sauce may also be lured into the business by the high profit margin. As a direct result, the supply of tomato sauce will most likely rise, the price will fall because of the expanded supply, and profit margins will then shrink. If profit margins shrink too much, supply may fall too far, and prices rise again. Throughout this trial and error process, consumers are signaling how much tomato sauce of what kind they want. Prices and profits relay their decisions.

The chief point to take away from all this is that the quest for profits in a competitive market increases supply. Increased supply in turn lowers, not raises prices. If profit is eliminated, prices will tend to rise, not fall. This is exactly what happened in France when government restricted the price of bread in order to make it more affordable. The result was that bread became much more expensive if it could be found at all.

The quest for profits also drives businesses to try to lower their costs—the prices they pay. The best way to lower business costs is to invest profits in equipment, facilities, or worker training. Businesses that fail to invest in order to lower their costs will soon find themselves losing out to competitors.

If a business succeeds in reducing its costs, this may increase profits, but usually not for long. Studies consistently show that over time the money saved by becoming more productive is used to increase worker pay or reduce consumer prices. Why? Because businesses have to compete for workers and customers and will lose them if they do not keep wages going up and consumer prices going down. Since workers are also consumers, rising wages with falling consumer prices is a formula for helping the average person.

If profits are not just temporarily high in an industry, but seem to be stuck for a long time at a high plateau, and no one seems to be manipulating or controlling prices, it tells us that there is some economic problem to be overcome, some bottleneck interfering with commerce. High profits then signal opportunity for the entrepreneur who can overcome the bottleneck.

For example, wheat was historically very difficult to get from farmer to market without spoiling or being eaten by rats, which enabled the hauler to charge high prices and earn a large profit. This eventually led entrepreneurs to invest in railroads and, later, trucks. Because these investments were successful, the cost of hauling wheat fell dramatically. From a free price system perspective, the temporarily high profit margins did their work. They attracted ingenuity and capital and the combination helped solve an economic problem.

Even Karl Marx, of all people, agreed that the profit system reduces prices. He stated as much in the *Communist Manifesto* of 1848:

> The cheap prices of its commodities are the heavy artillery with which [the profit system] compels all nations, on pain of extinction, to adopt the [profit] mode of production.[7]

4

Who Are the Bosses in a Free Price System?

MARX WAS RIGHT that profits drive down prices. But don't average people, and especially the poor, benefit from these lower prices? Why then did Marx say that the profit system is run by the rich for the benefit of the rich? Wasn't he being inconsistent, or at least confusing? If it is inconsistent or confusing to hold that profits drive down prices but nevertheless help the rich instead of the poor, why did history professor and contemporary Marxist Howard Zinn deepen the mystery further by arguing that

> the profit motive . . . has . . . distorted our whole economic and social system by making profit the key to what is produced.[8]

Economist Ludwig von Mises explains why Marx and Zinn are incorrect, why the free price (and profit) system especially benefits and ultimately is controlled by the many, not the few:

> Mass production [is] the fundamental principle of [profit-seeking] industry. . . . Big business, the target of the most fanatic attacks by the so-called leftists, produces . . . for the masses.[9]

Economist Milton Friedman develops this idea further:

> Progress . . . over the past century . . . has freed the masses from backbreaking toil and has made available to them products and services that were formerly the monopoly of the upper classes. . . .[10] The rich in Ancient Greece would have . . . welcomed the improvements in transportation and in medicine, but for the rest, the great achievements of [profit seeking] have redounded primarily to the benefit of the ordinary person.[11]

Henry Hazlitt is even more specific:

> The overwhelming majority of Americans . . . now enjoy the advantages of running water, central heating, telephones, automobiles, refrigerators, washing machines, [electronic

> music], radios, television sets—amenities
> that millionaires and kings did not enjoy
> a few generations ago.[12]

We must of course now add air conditioning and computers, which in some form are owned by a majority of poor people in America.

What about today's luxury goods? They represent a much smaller part of the economy than production for the masses, but cannot be said to benefit the masses. Or do they? Many of today's luxury goods will become tomorrow's necessities for everyone.

When luxuries first appear, they are almost always expensive; only people with considerable means can afford them. But as production grows, costs fall, so that more and more people, and eventually most people can afford them. This is how telephones, electricity, automobiles, and computers got their start as consumer items. If there had been no luxury buyers, such products would never have got a start, and no one would have them now.

Von Mises offers an additional point. Average consumers not only benefit from a free price (and profit) system. They also largely control it:

> Descriptive terms which people use are often quite misleading. In talking about modern captains of industry and leaders of big business, for instance, they call a man a

"chocolate king" or a "cotton king" or an "automobile king." Their use of such terminology implies that they see practically no difference between the modern heads of industry and those feudal kings, dukes or lords of earlier days. But the difference is in fact very great, for a chocolate king does not rule at all, he serves. This "king" must stay in the good graces of his subjects, the consumers; he loses his "kingdom" as soon as he is no longer in a position to give his customers better service and provide it at lower cost than others with whom he must compete.[13]

The concept of consumer economic control was articulated in 1928 by British economist Edwin Cannan. He wrote that

[some] try to convince the wage-earners that they are working not for the public and not for the consumers of the things or services which they produce, but for the capitalist employer, [but this is just] sour propaganda.[14]

Beatrice Potter, a founder with her husband Sidney Webb of Fabian Socialism, disputed Cannan:

In the business of my father everybody had to obey the orders issued by my father, the boss. He alone had to give orders, but to him nobody gave any orders.[15]

Ludwig von Mises in turn corrected Potter:

This is a very short-sighted view. Orders were given to her father by the consumers, by the buyers. Unfortunately [Potter] could not see these orders.[16]

5

"Spontaneous Order" from Free Prices

I N A FREE PRICE system, consumers as a whole are leading the economy. No one person or elite has much say about the direction we take. Some people find this disturbing. Will it not lead to chaos? Can any system thrive which is unguided, rudderless, subject to no visible commands? Will this not lead to trouble? The answer is quite simple: no.

A system led by consumers will produce by far the best outcome for consumers. Whom should an economy serve if not consumers? As we have noted, all workers are consumers, although not all consumers are workers. Our economic system should not revolve around the supposed needs of workers and certainly not around the supposed needs of business owners, but rather around the needs of consumers and then everyone, workers and business owners included, will benefit.

A system led by consumers is an example of what Michael Polanyi called a

spontaneous order.[17]

Some of our most important and reliable human systems work this way. For example, who directs human language? The French Academy tries to direct French, but no one pays much attention. Our common law has accumulated over the centuries in a similar way, unguided by any central leadership.

Social philosopher Walter Lippmann wrote of the

uncoordinated, unplanned, disorderly individualism[18]

of a free market economy, but he was wrong about it being unplanned. As economist Friedrich Hayek explained:

This is not a dispute about whether planning is to be done or not. It is a dispute as to whether planning is to be done centrally, by one authority for the whole economic system, or is to be divided among many individuals.[19]

Dividing economic leadership among billions of people creates a much more reliable and ordered system than any form of central control. It is also safer, because mistakes will be on a small scale, and therefore easily corrected, unlike the often catastrophic mistakes of central planners. The failure of the Soviet planners is a warning. So is President Franklin Roosevelt's failure to end the Great Depression. So is the Crash of 2008, primarily caused by US Federal Reserve and other central bank errors, which we will explore further in this book. Adam Smith explained this basic point in 1776:

> The statesman, who should attempt to direct private people in what manner they ought to employ their capitals, would not only load himself with a most unnecessary attention, but assume an authority which could safely be trusted, not only to no single person, but to no council or senate whatever, and which would nowhere be so dangerous as in the hands of a man who had folly and presumption enough to fancy himself fit to exercise it.[20]

6

What About Inequality?

THE FREE PRICE system produces unequal economic outcomes. About this, the economist John Maynard Keynes said that

> I want to mold a society in which most of the [economic] inequalities and causes of inequality are removed.[21]

Most people tend to agree with this—until they think through what it would mean to try to achieve it.

Consider, for example, the French Revolutionary slogan "liberty, equality, fraternity." On close inspection, there is something completely illogical about this. The ideals of liberty and equality are incompatible. If people are free, they will behave differently, which will lead to different outcomes. If I save and my friend does not, in the long run I should end up with a higher income, perhaps much higher. Should this be forbidden? And if so, how to forbid it? If government deprives us of liberty, ostensibly to enforce equality, as was done in the Soviet Union, the enforcers will themselves become a higher class with special privileges.

The enforcement of an ideology of equality has produced some of the most barbarous episodes in world history. Consider the story of a group of idealistic Americans from the Upper Midwest who in the 1930s decided that they did not want to live in a society propelled by "greed," but would instead volunteer their services in the "worker's paradise" of the Soviet Union. This led them to save, hire a boat, and embark for Russia.

On arrival, the volunteers were met by Soviet officials and were marched, perhaps singing Socialist songs, toward a work camp. There they were brutally enslaved and put to hard labor with little food and insufficient clothing or shelter to withstand the cold. Few are believed to have survived. Better known incidents include the massacre in Cambodia by Pol Pot of everyone with a degree of education, the extermination of the Kulaks by Stalin, and the Great Leap Forward and Cultural Revolution of Mao in China—in all of which many millions died.

To recognize that liberty and equality are logical opposites, or to cite such episodes, does not, however, make a complete argument against the desire to see a more equal society.

None of us want to see other people in need. Most of us think that we should try to help those who, for whatever reason, are suffering or living in abject poverty. The inescapable question is how best to do this. Is it to earn money and give a portion to charity, in addition to helping others get a start in the market system by hiring them? Or is it to restrict free prices and profits, or even to abolish the free price and profit system altogether?

To answer this, we will have to ask what works best. But we will also need to consider morality. American Socialist Michael Harrington has stated that

[the profit system] is outrageously unjust.

Is this right? Are incomes determined by the free price and profit system both

arbitrary

and

inequitable,

as John Maynard Keynes asserted?[22]

It is hard to see how our incomes are in any sense arbitrary. They are determined, like everything else in the free price system, by demand and supply. Norman Van Cott has explained that

> our incomes—be they large, small or some-
> where in between—reflect (1) our useful-
> ness to our fellow citizens and (2) the ease
> with which fellow citizens can find substi-
> tutes for us.[23]

It is natural to object that people are not commodities. But our labor is not our self. Our labor (unlike
our self) is a commodity and can be priced like any
other commodity. This is not unjust. It is reality.

It is also true that there is a large element of luck
in this. Some of us are indeed lucky to be born with
brains, to attend good schools, or even to inherit money.
All of these things make it easier to get more money.
But getting money is not the only, or even the most
important, way that we are lucky or unlucky. As economist Robert Sowell has noted:

> The difference between a factory worker
> and an executive is nothing compared to
> the difference between being born brain-
> damaged and being born normal, or the
> difference between being born to loving
> parents rather than abusive parents.[24]

If we are going to try to start leveling all the playing fields, where do we start? And how can we do it
without robbing people of their right to live life as
they see fit? For example, do you want everyone to

have the same medical care? Perhaps the same drug for the same malady? But is it the same malady, given our biological differences? Who will decide that? Or choose the drug? And on what basis? In the end, any such efforts defy common sense and logic as well as our right to make our own choices about ourselves.

Even if this is acknowledged, some will want to restrict free prices in an effort to reduce inequality, if only a bit. Economist Arthur Okun, a chairman of the President's Council of Economic Advisors during the 1960s, personally favored

complete [economic] equality,[25]

but thought that sacrificing some economic efficiency and growth for greater "equity" would be a reasonable compromise.

The trouble with this idea is that personal incomes are prices. When government tries to manipulate or control these prices, the result is not likely to be income redistribution. It is more likely to be wealth destruction.

Wealth is not something we pick up on the beach and share among ourselves. It has to be created through hard work, investment, insight, and oversight. Schemes of redistribution just destroy it for everyone, with particularly unfortunate consequences for the poor.

Another important point to keep in mind has been noted by economist Milton Friedman:

> Nowhere is the gap between rich and poor wider, nowhere are the rich richer and the poor poorer, than in those countries that do not permit the free market to operate.[26]

There is extensive evidence to support Friedman's assertion, including a notable World Bank study from economists David Dollar and Aart Kraay.[27]

7

The Essential Role of Loss and Bankruptcy

WE HAVE ALREADY noted that our incomes are objectively scored by the free price system, and that rich people can easily lose their incomes and assets if they make the wrong investment decisions. But there is a larger point to make here.

The entire price and profit system is objectively scored. You either make a profit or you suffer a loss. There is no ambiguity about it, provided that accounting is honest. And if you suffer large enough losses, you may go bankrupt. This is extremely important. As economist Wilhelm Röpke has explained:

> Since the fear of loss appears to be of more moment than the desire for gain, it may be

said that our economic system (in the final analysis) is regulated by bankruptcy.[28]

It is the special genius of the profit system that it per-
suades people to change or at least to accept change in
order to win a profit or to avoid a loss. Human beings
are often reluctant to accept change. Governments
and their bureaucracies are as a general rule notori-
ously unwilling to change.

Why does the United States still have 54,000 troops
in Germany in 2012, so many years after the end of
World War II and the Cold War with the Soviet Union?
Why is the once-thriving city of Detroit bankrupt, with
so many of its buildings boarded up or completely
abandoned? Why do government leaders promise to
balance their budgets, but fail to reach agreement on
how to do it and just keep falling deeper and deeper
in debt? Why is it that 136 years after the invention
of the telephone, it is estimated that half the world's
population has never used one?[29] The reason is that
governments, even democratic governments, do not
have any built in mechanism to force needed change,
as the profit system forces failing businesses to change.

Governments are also reinforced in their resistance to change by entrenched economic interests
that benefit from the status quo. It is the industries of
today, not the emerging industries of the future, that
have money to spend on elections and thus access to
government leaders. These entrenched interests use

all their influence with government to try to outlaw or at least slow down upstart competitors offering better ways of doing things.

Karl Marx recognized that the free price system pushes people to create or at least accept change. He did not like this and characterized it as

> uninterrupted disturbance of all social con-
> ditions, everlasting uncertainty and agi-
> tation. . . . All fixed, fast-frozen relations
> are swept away. . . . All that is solid melts
> into air.[30]

Well, perhaps, but economic growth assumes change. Without change, the human race would still be hunting and gathering. Very few of us would have been born or would have survived in such a precarious environment. Even so, at any given moment, the forces opposing change in a society are usually stronger than the forces favoring it.

Outside of a free price and profit system, the only way to achieve change is through government coercion. This is unlikely because, as noted, governments usually oppose change. Even in the few instances where a revolutionary government demands change, whether for good or ill, it is not usually able to bend people to its will for very long. Human beings devise passive-aggressive strategies to resist orders from above. Sheer terror, as practiced by Stalin, can overcome this kind of resistance for a time. But even the most brutal methods will ultimately falter, and how can an economy possibly innovate, grow, and thrive in a climate of fear and murder?

The most effective regulation is self-regulation, regulation that people voluntarily choose for themselves. The free price system is the prime example of a self-regulatory system and the greatest success story in human history. Through a combination of carrots and sticks, it leads people to want to make the changes that ultimately improve our standard of living. Price manipulations and controls by government are often described as regulations. But to the degree that they undermine the natural regulation of the free price system, they actually disregulate and destabilize our economic and social system.

8

Why Greed Is Not "Good" in a Free Price System

W**E HAVE ALREADY** seen that the price system encourages us to value, or at least accept, change, but it teaches us much more besides. It also teaches us to work hard, to defer gratification, to save rather than spend on ourselves. As a corollary of this, it encourages us to be patient, to keep our eyes fixed on the long term, not just the short term.

For example, if I start a business with $50,000 in initial sales and grow this at a fairly rapid 15% a year, it will take eighteen years to reach $400,000.

In another eighteen years, sales will reach $3.2 million; in another eighteen years, $25.6 million. If I survive for another eighteen years, I will see $205 million. As these numbers suggest, for a long time, the business will seem to be progressing at a snail's pace But if the growth rate can be maintained, the compounding of even larger numbers will produce stupendous returns. One more eighteen years to compound and the business will have grown to $1.6 billion in annual sales.

The founders of McDonald's and of Coca-Cola sold out in the first few years, and thus missed a chance to become enormously rich. The lesson is clear: have faith, stick with it, and do not let the first money you earn go to your head.

What else does the price system teach us? Critics say that it teaches us to be selfish and greedy. Is that true? The philosopher and novelist Ayn Rand, a famous defender of "free markets," would have answered: certainly, and a good thing at that.

Rand assumed that everyone is greedy, and that free markets directed aggression into constructive channels. This is not a new idea. Samuel Johnson, 18th century wise man and wit, suggested that

> there are few ways in which a man can be more innocently employed than in getting money.[31]

Economist John Maynard Keynes quipped

> it is better that a man tyrannize over his
> bank balance than over his fellow-citizens.[32]

Keynes was not a proponent of the "greed is good"
school, but did state that

> avarice and usury must be our gods for a little
> longer still. For only they can lead us out of the
> tunnel of economic necessity into daylight.[33]

18th century economist Adam Smith offered a
memorable defense—not of greed, but of rational
self-interest—when he declared that

> it is not from the benevolence of the butcher,
> the brewer, or the baker, that we expect our
> dinner, but from their regard to their own
> interest. We address ourselves, not to their
> humanity but to their self-love, and never
> talk to them of our own necessities but of
> their advantages.[34]

> . . . He generally, indeed, neither intends
> to promote the public interest, nor knows
> how much he is promoting it. . . . He in-
> tends only his own gain, and he is in this,
> as in many other cases, led by an invisible
> hand to promote an end which was no part
> of his intention.[35]

The motivational speaker Zig Ziglar turned this into some useful personal advice:

> You can have everything in life you want, if you'll just help enough other people get what they want.[36]

Adam Smith went on to argue that

> whenever commerce is introduced into any country, probity[,] punctuality[,] . . . economy, industry, [and] discretion . . . always accompany it. These virtues in a rude and barbarous country are almost unknown.[37, 38]

But, according to Smith, it is rational self-interest that promotes these personal and civic virtues.

Could Rand, Keynes, and even Smith be mistaken about the values taught by the free price system? Yes. This system is not teaching us to be greedy, or even directing that greed into more constructive channels. Nor is it only promoting rational self-interest. It is instead teaching us to stop thinking about our own needs and wishes and start focusing on the needs and wishes of others, in particular our employees and customers. If we try to do this only from rational self-interest, we will not find it easy. If we care genuinely about others, it will be much easier to stay the course, which typically is very long and demanding.

We have already seen that a "boss" of a successful business is not just a "boss," but rather a willing servant of others. Someone may "fake" this attitude for a while, but will ultimately be found out. Predation, exploitation, parasitism—all of these may augment the profits of a single transaction or a single year. But the worth of a business is defined as the "present value" of all future profits, and predatory practices do not amplify but rather destroy those future profits.

If a business owner must put the needs of employees and customers first, what about competitors? Is not market competition a cutthroat, dog-eat-dog business, with predation the rule rather than the exception? Once again, this is a false picture.

Most competition takes place within an organized, cooperative framework, similar to the Olympics. In some cases, competition is entirely collegial. Wheat farmers, for example, technically compete with one another, but think of themselves as colleagues, not competitors. In any case, there is only one durable way to out-compete other firms, and that is to serve your customers better and better. This is the only true competitive advantage—anything else is ephemeral.

Values inculcated by the free price system are demanding. They often take generations to learn. Once learned, they make the world, not only a more productive place, but a better place in which to live.

It is not surprising that proponents of the free price system led the battle against world slavery in the 18th and 19th centuries. And they were not only opposed to slavery. They were also opposed to nationalism, tribalism, racism, and sectarianism as well.

The free price system teaches us to tolerate, work with, and ultimately appreciate people of all lands and conditions. If we do not, we will lose our best employees and many potential customers. As noted before, this is not just a matter of calculation. Either we believe it or we do not. In the long run, people will not be fooled.

Economist George Stigler understands all this:

> Important as the moral influences of the marketplace are, they have not been subjected to any real study. The immense proliferation of general education, of scientific progress, and of democracy are all coincidental in time and place with the emergence of the free enterprise system of organizing the marketplace. I believe this coincidence was not accidental.[39]

Economist Geoffrey Martin Hodgson does not understand free price system values:

> The firm has to compete not simply for profit but for our confidence and trust.

> To achieve this, it has to abandon profit-
> maximization, or even shareholder satis-
> faction, as the exclusive objectives of the
> organization.[40]

This is hopelessly wrong. The only way we can maximize profits is to earn the confidence and trust of our customers. These two activities are not mutually exclusive. They are one and the same.

Economist John Kenneth Galbraith, past president of the American Economic Association, and best-selling author, also demonstrates a complete lack of understanding when he writes that

> there is nothing reliable to be learned about
> making money. If there were, study would
> be intense and everyone with a positive IQ
> would be rich.[41]

But it is not a high IQ, or a business degree, that enables us to make money. It is a strong desire to serve others, along with sound judgment about how to go about it, since, in business as in life, good intentions are not enough.

Part 3

How Central Banking Threatens the Free Price System

9

The Puzzle of Central Banking

Some of the basic principles we have covered in Parts 1 and 2 include:

- Free prices enable an economy to function honestly, efficiently, and productively.
- The free price system drives down the cost of almost everything. This particularly helps the poor.
- The free price system regulates human conduct more effectively than anything else. Governments should take care that laws support rather than dismantle this natural, voluntary, and powerful regulatory system.

- Loss and bankruptcy, not just profit, are critical features of the free price regulatory system.
- Profit and loss together persuade people to seek change or to accept change. Without change, we would still be hunting and gathering and very few of us would be alive. Governments tend to oppose change, and lack any effective mechanism to bring it about.
- The economy should be run by and for consumers, not by and for elite planners.
- The free price system teaches important moral lessons which are as important for our society as our economy.

Having listed these principles, all of which accord with common sense, we now confront a puzzle. Most countries, the US included, have delegated day-to-day control of their money, and much of the management of their economy, to central banks. Given the immense power these institutions possess, why do they intentionally thwart all the principles cited above? Why do they:

- Distort all prices?
- Fail to recognize the consequences of the inflation they promote by distorting the free price system?
- Engage in outright fixing of some of the most important prices, thereby blowing up bubble/bust cycles?

- Refuse to allow economy-wide prices to fall, particularly hurting the poor?
- Refuse to let loss and bankruptcy do their work in regulating the economy as a whole?
- Create rules that destroy free prices in banking and thus destroy the banking system's ability to regulate itself?
- Substitute the judgment of elite planners for that of consumers, despite the dismal economic record of central planning?
- Serve the interests of politicians and private parties allied with politicians rather than the public?
- Devalue and destroy important moral standards taught by the free price system?
- Stretch or ignore the law governing their operations with seeming impunity?

In the rest of this section, we shall address each question in turn.

10

The US Federal Reserve and Prices

AS WE SAW in Chapter 3, a free price system drives consumer prices down, not up. It gives us a gradual reduction in prices, exactly what we should want. Falling prices are the payoff for learning to produce goods and services more and more productively.

Innovation and productivity, along with accompanying price reductions, are the essence of economic progress. They are especially helpful to the poor, who can buy more and more with limited means. For everyone, but especially for the poor, rising prices are a threat, and also an admission of economic failure.

For most of the decades prior to the founding of the Fed, US prices fell more often than they rose. There were exceptions—particularly the sharp inflation during and after the Civil War—but prices did not stay high. During the last decades of the 19th century, prices trended down. During that period, the US economy expanded so dramatically that it became the wonder of the world. Stock prices also advanced. A study of stock prices since 1872 found that the best returns in US history came during a period of mild deflation (gradually falling consumer prices).[42]

Two years after the Fed began operation in 1914, consumer price inflation soared. Since the Fed was charged with controlling inflation, this was not a good harbinger for the future, but was excused on the grounds that World War I had to be financed, and this required a suspension of the usual rules. The Fed statute was amended to give the organization more "flexibility" and inflation continued. By 1920, prices had doubled, then fell sharply in the Depression of 1920–1921, recovered, fell for the rest of the decade, plunged again following the 1929 Crash. After that prices only rose, especially during the 1960s and 1970s.

At the end of the 1970s, Fed Chairman Paul Volcker acted vigorously to rein in what was becoming a runaway inflation, and for a time succeeded. But in the quarter century following, consumer prices doubled again. At that point, Volcker conceded:

> If the overriding objective is price stabil-
> ity, we did a better job with the nineteenth
> century gold standard and passive central
> banks, with currency boards or even "free
> banking."[43]

As the Fed's first century approached, the dollar had lost a stunning 97% of its purchasing power. A consumer in 2012 needed $33 to buy what one dollar would have bought in 1914. Millionaires, defined as people with a net worth of $1 million dollars, were no longer even classed as "rich."

By then, Fed Chairman Ben Bernanke was operating with an explicit "2% inflation target," which meant that he wanted 2% inflation a year. What were the implications of this? Assume for a moment that half of the economy is highly productive (think of computers) and is reducing its prices by 3% a year, not an unreasonable figure. If so, how much inflation will be needed from the less productive half of the economy to arrive at an overall total of 2%? The answer is 7% (2% is midway between -3 and 7).

The Bernanke doctrine thus demands that a large portion of the economy operate at a highly unproductive rate. Viewed in this light, it seems illogical. Why would anyone want this outcome? Nor was it improved when the Fed chairman announced in late 2012 that he was raising the upper boundary of "acceptable" inflation to 2.5%.

It is also important to recognize that government statistics about the rate of inflation have become increasingly unreliable. Under the Reagan administration, some government payments, especially Social Security checks to retirees, were tied to the Consumer Price Index (CPI) calculated by the Commerce Department. Since then, the method of calculating the CPI has been modified, especially during the Clinton administration. Without these changes, which reduced CPI growth and therefore reduced the amount owed retirees by the federal government, the total loss of purchasing power during recent years would look far worse.[44] The Fed, it is true, does not primarily rely on the CPI, as most observers do. But the series it does use is no more reliable.

Ironically, the Fed's preference for its own inflation index in itself tends to depress CPI reported inflation. This is because the Fed's favored measure of inflation excludes food and energy prices. If Fed policies drive up the cost of these items, consumers will have less money to spend on items other than food and energy. Reduced spending on these items will then help to lower prices which the Fed acknowledges and watches. In this way, the Fed can claim that inflation is falling when prices as a whole are clearly rising. When consumers are asked in surveys which prices matter the most to them, they generally mention food and energy. But the Fed is not paying attention.

Meanwhile American consumers have increasingly relied on cheap foreign goods bought, in many instances, with borrowed money supplied by the sellers. In 1991, only 15% of US consumer expenditures went to foreign producers. Fifteen years later, this had risen to 40%.[45] Cheap foreign goods provided on easy terms were not likely to push up the standard US consumer price indexes.

Regardless of how inflation is measured, and no matter what the standard indexes miss, there is no disputing that there has been massive consumer price inflation during the Fed's century long stewardship of the economy. Why is this? Has it been despite the Fed's best efforts or rather because of the Fed? To get to the bottom of this question, we must first ask what causes inflation.[46]

A popular idea is that prices rise when an economy grows too fast and becomes "overheated." But economic growth means that more goods and services are being produced. This increase in supply, as noted previously, should tend to reduce, not increase prices.

By far the most important reason that prices rise and stay high is that government has "printed"* new money and injected it into the economy—either directly or through the banking system. As the amount of money

---

* This refers to electronic means of creating money, not just printing of paper bills.

circulating rises relative to the supply of goods and services, the price of those goods and services expressed in
dollars naturally rises.

A simple example may help make this clear. If the
economy consisted entirely of two knives and $2, it
would be logical for each knife to be priced at $1. But
if the amount of money doubles to $4, without any
more knives being produced, the price of each of the
two existing knives would be expected to rise to $2.
Economist Milton Friedman summed this up in a
famous passage:

> Just as an excessive increase in the quan-
> tity of money is the one and only impor-
> tant cause of inflation, so a reduction in
> the rate of monetary growth is the one and
> only cure for inflation.[47]

The Federal Reserve is responsible for the quantity
of money in the US, so it follows that the Fed is responsible for the dollar's collapse in purchasing power since
1914. As economist Murray Rothbard has noted:

> If the chronic inflation undergone by Amer-
> icans, and in almost every other country, is
> caused by the continuing creation of new
> money, and if in each country its govern-
> mental "central bank" (in the United States,
> the Federal Reserve) is the sole monopoly
> source and creator of all money, who then

> is responsible for the blight of inflation?
> Who except the very institution that is
> solely empowered to create money, that is,
> the Fed (and the Bank of England, and the
> Bank of Italy, and other central banks)? . . .
> In short . . . the Fed and the banks are not
> part of the solution to inflation. . . . In fact,
> they are the problem.[48]

It must be noted that the Fed since 1977 has had a so-called dual mandate from Congress: control inflation but also promote "full" employment. This complicates the picture. But, even so, given the explicit charge to control inflation, and the actual record of creating massive amounts of it, why does Congress do nothing about the situation? Congress established the Fed and retains ultimate authority over money, so why not step in and fix the problem? Thibault de Saint Phalle, author of *The Federal Reserve: An Intentional Mystery*, explains that

> no one in Congress ever points out . . . it
> is the Fed itself that creates inflation. [The
> reason for this is that] the Fed, by financing
> the federal deficit year after year, makes it
> possible for Congress to continue to spend
> far more than it collects in tax revenues. If it
> were not for Fed action, Congress would have
> to curb its spending habits dramatically.[49]

What exactly does de Saint Phalle mean by this? How does the Fed help finance government deficit spending when it creates new money? In most cases, this is done indirectly.

The government borrows money by selling a bond, let us say to a bank. The Federal Reserve then buys the bond from the bank with newly "printed" money. In effect, the government sells a bond to itself, but very few people understand what is happening.

Most people believe that the largest creditors of the US government, buyers of its bonds, are the Japanese and Chinese governments. This is not correct. The largest owner of US government bonds is the US government itself, operating through the Federal Reserve.

A government is expected to finance itself through taxes. Historically, governments hard up for money have also created new currency to spend. In the 1920s, Germany simply printed new marks. If a central bank buys in a government bond, it is the functional equivalent of printing new currency. Whatever method is used—taxes, currency printing, or buying in bonds— the result is to transfer resources from the private sector to government.

To see this more clearly, assume that an economy consists of $1 and miscellaneous goods and services. Government may either levy 25¢ in taxes or "print" 33.3¢ in new money for its own use. Either way government now has the wherewithal to command

25% of all economy-wide goods and services. (25¢ is a quarter of $1.00 and 33.3¢ is a quarter of $1.00 plus 33.3¢.) Private businesses and individuals are left with 75%.

Even if governments do not create money in order to finance their own deficits directly, an expansion of the money supply will still enable them to borrow more. This is because rising consumer prices steadily reduce the real value of the debt. If I lend $1,000 to anyone, the borrower gets $1,000 in purchasing power. If the borrower repays me after twenty years, and there has been inflation of a little over 3.5% a year in the interim, I only get back $500 in purchasing power.

The US government is fully aware that inflation allows the borrower to slip out of contractual debt without default. As federal debt exploded following the Crash of 2008, it became clear that the Bernanke Fed hoped to inflate away the massive debt, but to do so slowly enough to avoid setting off alarms among lenders. Alarms among lenders would be potentially disastrous, since it could lead to spiraling interest rates.

Like the federal government, Wall Street also benefits from the Fed's proclivity to "print" more and more money. Most of this new money passes through Wall Street on its way to wherever it is going in the economy, and in transit fattens Wall Street profits. In addition, although some of the money enters the consumer economy, where it raises consumer prices, much of it enters investment markets, where it raises the prices of stock, bonds, or real estate. Wall Street generally benefits from rising asset prices, as well as from all the speculation triggered by the new money.

Average people, of course, do not own many assets. The poor own fewest of all, so they do not benefit from asset price increases and speculation. On the contrary, they suffer from it when they try to buy a car or first home and find that the cost of the car or home has been inflated beyond their means.

11

Prices, Bubbles, and Busts

A s noted earlier, free prices provide clear and vital information to all market participants. This information enables participants continually to adjust supply and demand and thus bring them into balance. By contrast, rising prices engineered by government send mixed and confusing messages.

New government money pours into the economy in completely unpredictable ways, entering first this sector, then another, distorting prices as it goes. If new money flows into computers, it will seem that demand for computers has increased, but this is a false signal. If it flows into housing, builders may increase production in the mistaken belief that consumer preferences really have shifted to houses. This is what happened during the US housing bubble leading up to the Crash of 2008, but it is not a new phenomenon. Economist John Stuart Mill described how this works in the early 19th century:

> An increase of production . . . takes place during the progress of [money expansion], as long as the existence of [money expansion] is not suspected. . . . But when the delusion vanishes and the truth is disclosed, those whose commodities are relatively in excess must diminish their production or be ruined: and if during the high prices they have built mills and erected machinery, they will be likely to repent at leisure.[50]

Economist Ludwig von Mises provided the earliest systematic explanation of how bubbles blow up, filled with the helium of new government money, and then burst in his 1912 book *The Theory of Money and Credit*. Mises's student Henry Hazlitt summarized the process:

> [Governments injecting too much money into the economy create] unbalanced production, misdirected production, production of the wrong things . . .[51] which in turn creates unemployment and malemployment.[52]

What is malemployment (also called sub-optimal employment)? This is a very important concept discussed by economist W. H. Hutt. It reminds us that people not only need work, they need the right work, work that will make the best use of their unique skills, work that will last. People pulled into housing trades during a housing bubble may count as employed, but it is sub-optimal employment.

Human nature, our tendency toward greed or fear, what economist John Maynard Keynes and followers such as Robert Shiller have called "animal spirits," certainly played a role in creating the record of bubble and bust. But human nature, whatever it is, remains a constant. What changes is the amount of new money made available to Wall Street by central banks. When the spigot is open, bubbles form. The new money is not of course given away. It is lent. And once the debt exceeds the capacity to repay, the bubble bursts and millions of people lose their jobs, as they did in the Depression of 1920, the Great Depression, the Crash of 2008, and in other recessions such as the one that followed the Dot Com bubble in 2000.

About the Crash of 2008, President George W. Bush said that

Wall Street got drunk.

This is true enough, but Wall Street does not get drunk all the time. It was "free drinks" from the Federal

Reserve under chairmen Alan Greenspan and Ben Bernanke that explain the timing of the binge.

In view of the Fed's record, it is remarkable that economic writer Jeffrey Madrick should have written that

> by 1913 the US federal government created a stable financial system with the creation of the Federal Reserve.[53]

Whether measured by price stability or employment stability, the record of the Fed has been utterly dismal.

It is not that bubbles and busts did not exist before the Fed. For as long as governments have controlled money, which is to say for thousands of years, there have been such incidents. But, as economist Gottfried Haberler observed:

> During the second half of the nineteenth century there was a marked tendency for [economic] disturbances to become milder. Especially those conspicuous events, breakdowns, bankruptcies, and panics became less numerous, and there were even business cycles from which they were entirely absent. Before [WWI], it was the general belief of economists that ... dramatic breakdowns and panics ... belonged definitely to the past.[54]

Milton Friedman has been even more critical:

The severity of each of the major contractions—1920–1921, 1929–1933, and 1937–1938—is directly attributable to acts of commission and omission by the Reserve authorities and would not have occurred under earlier monetary and banking arrangements.[55]

12

Price Fixing Follies 1

S O FAR, WE have discussed how consumer and asset price inflation have surged under the Fed, how the Fed's excessive creation of money has fueled the inflation, and how this has distorted most prices, with often disastrous consequences for employment. But the Fed does not just distort prices in general.

Economic writer Gene Callahan has charged that

> [the chairman of the Federal Reserve] is the head price fixer of a price fixing agency.[56]

Callahan is not exaggerating. As part of the process of "managing" money, the Fed either fixes outright or seeks to manipulate some of the most important prices in the economy.

At the present time, the Fed fixes the so-called Fed Funds Rate, the key short-term interest rate. Because long-term interest rates are in practice an aggregation of shorter-term rates, fixing short rates strongly influences long rates. Moreover, the Bernanke Fed has tried to move long-term interest rates (down) more directly by buying longer-term bonds with its newly created money. It has also tried to put a lid on mortgage interest rates. And it has publicly acknowledged seeking to put a floor under stock prices by keeping interest rates low, a step which, as we have already noted, tends to make the rich richer.[57]

Most of this is taken from the playbook of the British economist John Maynard Keynes. In his *General Theory*, Keynes wrote that

> the rate of interest is not self-adjusting at a level best suited to the social advantage but constantly tends to rise too high. . . .[58] [Interest] rates . . . have been [too high] for the greater part of recorded history.[59]

There are few facts and little logic to support Keynes's assertion. But it does tell us something important: that he does not trust the free price system. He thinks that he will do better at choosing appropriate rates than market participants, acting together, and today's central bankers work from exactly the same premise.

Moreover, interest rates are pivotal prices. They represent the cost of money, or more precisely, the cost of credit, that is, the cost of borrowing. Money is involved in most economic transactions, and credit in many of them. If someone is determined to destroy the free price system, distorting interest rates is a sure place to start.

Artificially low interest rates tempt both business and consumers to borrow for unsound reasons. Prior to the take-off of the US housing bubble of the early 2000s, the Fed kept its Fed Funds Rate below the rate of official inflation for several years. This was virtually giving money away. As Peter R. Fisher, former under-secretary of the US Treasury and New York Federal Reserve Bank official, has explained:

> Capitalism is premised on the idea that capital is a scarce commodity, and we are going to ration it with a price mechanism. When you make short-term funds [available] essentially free with negative real rates [rates lower than inflation, as happened for example 2001–2004], crazy things start to happen.[60]

When the housing bubble blew up with the Crash of 2008, the Fed reduced its key interest rate even further to one quarter of one percent, as close to free money as could be achieved. Some Keynesian economists were not satisfied with this. They

wanted the Fed to drive up consumer price inflation well past its 2% target, to as high as 6%. This
would make the real (inflation-adjusted) short-term
interest rate as low as -5.75% (6% inflation minus the
negligible .25% interest rate). In effect, the borrower
would be paid to borrow rather than the lender paid
to lend, an inversion of common sense that is typical
of Keynesian ideas.

This curious notion of paying the borrower to borrow was promoted by two economists allied with
the Republican Party, Greg Mankiw, former chairman of President George W. Bush's Council of Economic Advisors and advisor to presidential candidate
Mitt Romney, and his Harvard colleague Ken Rogoff.[61] Mankiw declined to say how much repression
of interest rates would be optimal while his colleague
filled in more details. Rogoff's endorsement was
somewhat unexpected given his earlier quip about
the Crash of 2008 and its aftereffects:

> We borrowed too much, we screwed up, so
> we're going to fix it by borrowing more.[62]

Exactly how would paying borrowers to borrow
help clean up all the bad loans from a housing bubble
that had been engineered in the first place by similar
Fed inducements for borrowers to borrow?

The Bernanke Fed, Mankiw, and Rogoff were
ignoring the advice of economist Ludwig von Mises,

who, as we have noted, had worked out the primary reason for crashes a century earlier:

> Boom . . . , followed by . . . depression, is the unavoidable outcome of the attempts, repeated again and again, to lower the gross market rate of interest by means of [money and] credit expansion.[63]

What Mises meant was that the Fed, hoping to "stimulate" the economy, tries to lower interest rates by creating new money to be lent. The result may be "stimulating" in the short term, but sews the seeds of economic destruction.

Mises's student Henry Hazlitt summed up the Mises analysis:

> If one truth concerning economic crises has been established . . . it is that they are typically brought on by cheap money— i.e., low interest rate policies that encourage excessive borrowing, excessive credit expansion, imprudent speculation, and all the distortions and instabilities in the economy that these finally bring about.[64]

Keynes's rejoinder, also from *The General Theory,* is that

> the remedy for the boom is not a higher rate of interest but a lower rate of interest!

> For that may enable the boom to last. The
> right remedy for the trade cycle is not to be
> found in abolishing booms and thus keep-
> ing us permanently in a semi-slump: but
> in abolishing slumps and thus keeping us
> permanently in a quasi-boom.[65]

The Bernanke Fed in effect followed this advice in 2007. It lowered the Fed Funds Rate in an attempt to rescue the economy as it teetered toward the Crash of 2008. This almost immediately backfired. It persuaded Wall Street to take one last, big gulp of leverage (debt) at just the wrong moment. It also set off a round of speculation in commodities as investors sought to protect themselves from infla-tion and a falling dollar. The price of oil doubled in only a few months, which further added to the economic strain.

Bernanke compounded his error on interest rates by seeking to modify banking rules in an unreal-istic way, which will be discussed in a later chapter. The combination of interest rate and banking errors accelerated the Crash. But for Bernanke's actions, the Crash might have come a year or two later, after the Bush presidency had ended. If so, we would not have heard President Bush say on television:

> I've abandoned free market principles to
> save the free market system,[66]

something the president had presumably heard from his economic advisors, but which they had probably not intended for public consumption.

A Keynesian policy of forcing interest rates down assumes that more debt will always help the economy. Common sense tells us, on the contrary, that debt will not be effective unless used prudently and intelligently. Borrowing and lending decisions must be guided by free prices, not by academic economists working at the Fed. There is some evidence that the return on debt in the US economy has been declining for decades. During the decade 1950–1959, each dollar of new debt produced 73¢ in economic growth, according to government figures. For the decade 1990–1999, this fell to 31¢. For the eight years prior to the Crash of 2008, it fell to 19¢, and it has likely been negative since.[67]

Although common sense tells us that debt must be in the right hands, used for the right purposes, in the right amount, Keynesian economists George Akerlof and Robert Shiller have proposed that the US government develop a target each year for total economy-wide borrowing and then take whatever actions will push borrowing to that level.[68] In effect, these economists, closely allied with the Keynesians inside the Fed, believe that we should start with the amount we want to borrow, not with how it will be used or by whom.

What none of these economists even try to explain
is how debt can grow, year after year, at a faster rate
than underlying economic growth. Economist Marc
Faber points out the inescapable truth:

> When debt growth vastly exceeds nomi-
> nal GDP [gross domestic product] growth,
> sooner or later something will have to give.[69]

In a sound economy, the Fed would heed 19th century French economist Jean-Baptiste Say's injunction
that

> [the] rate of interest ought no more to be re-
> stricted, or determined by law, than . . . the
> price of wine, linen, or any other commodity.[70]

It would then stop promoting promiscuous borrowing and spending. It would stop discouraging saving and allow people to make their own decisions
about these matters. It would stop preventing people from earning income on their savings or forcing
savers to take more and more risk in order to produce any income.

Businesses would in turn borrow those savings and
put them to work in innovative or productivity-
enhancing projects. The watchword would be quality of investment, not just quantity, in complete contrast to the Keynesian approach followed by the Fed.
Each step of the way, consumers, savers, investors, and

entrepreneurs would be guided by the truthful and useful information contained in free prices.

13

Price Fixing Follies 2

THE PRINCIPAL PRICES fixed or influenced by the US Fed are interest rates. But decisions reached about interest rates, credit, or overall quantity of money also strongly influence the price of the US dollar in world markets.

Some other central banks operate differently. They may try to control the value of their country's currency and only secondarily try to influence interest rates. For technical reasons that need not concern us here, it is not possible for a central bank to fix both a currency price and a base interest rate. Central banks must choose.

When central banks choose to concentrate on currency, they usually want either to drive the price down or hold it down. Why? Because they believe that this will make their country's goods cheaper on world markets, which will "stimulate" exports, which will help create more jobs, which will help the country's government hang on to power.

Does any of this work? It may for a time. But if most other countries are playing the same game, even short-term gains may not materialize. Moreover, driving the price of your currency down makes imports more expensive, which drives up costs for the middle class and poor as well as for businesses and eventually for consumers as a whole. It will even hit exporters insofar as they depend on imported components. As Paul Volcker, former Fed chairman, has said:

> A depreciating currency [leaves] the nation poorer, not richer, . . . not something to jump with joy about.[71]

Steve Roach, former Morgan Stanley chief economist adds:

> I have looked at economic history back to the Babylonian era, and there has never been a country that has prospered on the back of a weak currency.[72]

There is an even darker side to central bank devaluation of currencies. These manipulations have now replaced tariffs (taxes on imported goods) as the preferred form of protectionism. Whatever form it takes, protectionism is just another form of price control, in this case intended to raise the price of foreign goods and thus prevent them from competing with domestic goods.

Most economists agree that the US Smoot-Hawley Tariff Act, which substantially raised taxes on foreign goods shortly after the Crash of 1929, crippled foreign trade and by doing so deepened the Depression. As Llewellyn Rockwell, chairman of the Ludwig von Mises Institute, has noted:

> The tragedy of [protectionism, whether through tariffs or competitive currency devaluation] is that it tends to creep up when it can do the most damage, that is, during economic downturns.[73]

Just as Rockwell would have expected, currency manipulation by central banks significantly increased after the Crash of 2008.

Global markets are an integral part of the free price system. Left undistorted by government price controls, including protectionism, they can contribute greatly to the elimination of world poverty. One of the reasons that the United States prospered so much in its brief history is that it had a very large market, unencumbered by internal tariffs or other trade barriers. A fully integrated global economy can be even more successful than a large national market.

The central concept behind global trade is usually known as "comparative advantage." It states that a country should concentrate on what it does best, let other countries do the same, and then trade with others to supply what is missing. This works even if one country does everything best.

Economist Thomas Sowell illustrates the math of the concept in his book *Basic Economics*. Assume, hypothetically, that the US makes shirts twice as cheaply and shoes 25% more cheaply than Canada. Should the US then make its own shirts and shoes? No. As Sowell demonstrates, if the US makes all the shirts and Canada all the shoes, the total production of shirts and shoes for the two countries increases by approximately 20% and 11% respectively. The bottom line is that allowing imports makes everyone better off, including workers directed to more productive, and therefore better paying, jobs.

This same principle applies to the "outsourcing" of service jobs over telephone or internet lines. Outsourcing eliminates some US jobs. But it may also allow a US based company to reduce its overall costs, and thus to stay in business. If "outsourcing" were illegal, the company might not be able to compete at all, which would entail the loss of many more, and probably better paying, jobs.

All forms of protectionism, including the modern form of currency devaluation, are ultimately self-defeating. The early 19th century British reformer Richard Cobden had the right answer:

> I hold all idea of regulating the currency to be an absurdity. . . . The currency . . . must be regulated by the trade and commerce of the world; I would neither allow the Bank of England nor any private banks to have what is called the management of the currency.[74]

14

Why Falling Prices Are What We Should Want

WHAT EXACTLY DOES the Fed have against falling prices? We explained in Chapter 3 and elsewhere that falling prices are a principal payoff of the free price system. As prices fall, everyone benefits, especially the poor, since they have the least money.

The steel magnate Andrew Carnegie said that the market's job is to turn luxuries into necessities. By necessities, he meant articles that were low enough in price to be afforded by most businesses or consumers, not just the wealthy ones. The steel that Carnegie himself produced was a good example. He found ways to make it more and more productively, that is more and more cheaply, so that he could charge lower and lower prices and find more and more customers. Consumers did not buy this steel, but other producers did, and those producers could then sell more cheaply to consumers.

Carnegie became the richest man in America by selling steel at ever lower prices, but that was only the most visible part of the story. As companies in other industries were able to buy steel cheaply, that meant that they could become more productive themselves and sell their own goods more cheaply. For example, more railroads could be built at lower prices, so that the cost of railroad freight and travel fell. Since agricultural and other products were shipped by rail, this reduced their prices. The cost of drilling wells and transporting oil also fell, so that oil and gasoline became cheaper and more widely available. Office skyscrapers could be built for the first time, so office space became cheaper and more available. As Carnegie said, this is what markets are supposed to do: increase productivity and lower prices, which leads to more productivity and even lower prices.

The Fed (and other central banks) will allow some of this, but not very much. It hews dogmatically to the illogical doctrine that deflation, a general fall in prices throughout the economy, is dangerous and must be prevented at all cost. Why? The worry is that even a mild deflation might tip the economy over into a sudden, deep deflation, the kind that is associated with depressions.

This is a complete confusion of cause and effect. Depressions are not caused by collapsing prices. Rather collapsing prices are caused by depressions. The real source of crashes and depressions is to be found in the bubbles that precede them, and these bubbles for the last century have usually been engineered by the Fed itself in its misguided efforts to thwart naturally falling prices.

The Fed currently wants at least 2% inflation as a kind of "insurance" against any deflation at all. As previously noted, if the economy, left alone, might produce prices declining by 2% a year, this means that the Fed must gin up a great deal of inflation in large swaths of the economy to reach its overall 2% inflation target. This policy is intended to keep the economy on a more stable path, but actually produces the exact opposite. German economist Wilhelm Röpke has noted that

> the more stabilization [by the Fed] the less stability.[75]

Austrian economist Friedrich Hayek makes the same point:

> The more we try to provide full security by interfering with the market system, the greater the insecurity becomes.[76]

As the Fed lowers interest rates by pouring new money into the economy, seeking thereby to prevent a general price decline, economic bubbles begin to inflate. These bubbles are, in turn, followed by bust. Nothing could be more ironic: the Fed, by the very actions it hopes will forestall depression, actually brings it on.

15

How Dr. Fed Makes the Patient Sicker 1

WHEN AN ECONOMIC bust arrives, following the bubble previously blown up by Fed action, what does the master planner do? It just doubles down, lowers interest rates further, floods the economy with even more money, all in the hope that it can generate even more borrowing and spending. How can anyone think that this will work?

After the Crash of 2008, Ben Bernanke said that his actions were designed

to solve this problem.[77]

But if too much bad debt is the problem, how will piling on more debt solve it? If large amounts of money have been wasted on unwise borrowing and spending, why will it help to waste even more? Economist Friedrich Hayek has noted that

> to combat the depression by [printing more money and encouraging more debt] is to attempt to cure the evil by the very means which brought it about.[78]

Hayek continues:

> The same stabilizers who believed that nothing was wrong with the boom and that it might last indefinitely because [consumer] prices did not rise, now believe that everything could be set right again if only we would use the weapons of monetary policy to prevent prices from falling.[79]

> … Instead of furthering the inevitable liquidation of the maladjustments brought about by the boom during the [prior] years, all conceivable means have been used to prevent that readjustment from taking place….[80]

When the inflationary bubble fueled by the Fed during World War I burst in the Depression of 1920–1921, the Fed had not yet fully developed its current methods, and chose not to intervene to prop up prices. Both prices and the economy plunged precipitously, but then righted themselves and recovered.

The Depression was over in only a year and a half, in sharp contrast to what happened after the Crash of 1929. In 1920–1921, the Fed actually raised interest rates while the Harding administration cut government spending dramatically in order to balance the budget. All of this is directly contrary to current Fed (Keynesian) doctrine, but the record speaks for itself. By 1923, unemployment in the US was only 2.4%.[81]

During the 1920s, Benjamin Strong, head of the New York Fed, developed some of the present credit expansion techniques ("open market policy"), in order to "stimulate" and "manage" the economy. In 1927, the boom (actually bubble) seemed to be faltering, so Strong decided to

> give a little coup de whiskey to the stock market.[82]

This miscalculation, like Ben Bernanke's lowering of interest rates in 2007, contributed to the Crash that followed.

After the Crash of 1929, first President Hoover and then President Roosevelt acted vigorously to prevent employers from reducing wages. Wages are of course among the most important prices of the economy. Since the final price of goods was plunging, an inability to reduce wages meant that many companies faced almost certain bankruptcy. The only way to prevent this was to lay off employees on a massive scale.

Ironically, those employees not laid off got the equivalent of enormous raises. The reason was that pre-crash wages, in effect frozen by the government, could buy much more because of the then reduced prices of all consumer goods. In this way, some, especially unionized workers supported by the Roosevelt administration, got a windfall while millions of others became homeless or went hungry.

Following World War II, many people, including many economists, expected the economy to fall back into depression. They argued against ending wartime price and wage controls and also against reducing government expenditure and taxes. Fortunately this advice was not followed. General price and wage controls were abandoned, government spending was cut 70% by 1948, joint income tax filing was introduced, which at that time reduced income taxes, and many business and excise taxes were eliminated.

As a result, the return of 10 million veterans did not drive up unemployment. This remained below 5% until the recession of 1949 temporarily raised it to 6%. These figures were far, far better than anything achieved by the Keynesian policies employed before the war during the Great Depression.[83]

Today we no longer hear anyone calling for the US government to hold up wages during an economic downturn, as was done so destructively during the Great Depression. That is because government will print enough new money to prevent any general price decline, including a decline in wages. And the same policy is followed in most developed countries.

The monumental crash of Japan in the late 1980s following an earlier bubble is particularly instructive, because that crash presaged later crashes in the US and Europe, and because the Japanese government followed standard Keynesian doctrine in its response. Several decades later, the Japanese economy is still depressed, and so much new government debt has been created that tax receipts barely cover debt service (even at artificially repressed interest rates) and social security payments.

In sharp contrast, other Asian economies that crashed in the late 1990s side-stepped the standard Keynesian "remedies" and recovered swiftly. Their example should have been studied more closely. Following the Crash of 2008, most countries ignored it and sought to apply the standard Keynesian remedies of printing money and piling new bad debt on old. Only a few, such as Latvia and Estonia, did not, and they have relatively low unemployment today.[84]

Despite all this historical evidence, central bankers still do not understand that their own actions, meant to keep prices up, are simply blowing up bubbles, causing crashes, and then setting the stage for even worse crashes. They speak of "buying time" and "restoring confidence." They also continue to promote the long discredited idea of Keynes's that crashes, left alone, may free fall and fail ever to find a bottom, or plateau at an unacceptably high level of unemployment.

President Obama echoed this fallacy when he said in early 2009 that

> the failure to act, and act now, will turn a crisis into a catastrophe. [Without government intervention,] at some point we may not be able to reverse [the] crisis.[85]

This was identical to Keynes's statement that a contracting economy, left alone, could lose the

> capacity for rebound.[86]

None of this is true, and Keynesians should know it. Keynes's own disciple, celebrated economist Franco Modigliani, demonstrated the faultiness of this reasoning in a 1944 paper, two years before Keynes's death. Modigliani and others reaffirmed the classical idea that unemployment is telling us that prices are out of balance. The role of markets is precisely to balance prices, so that it is fallacious to suggest that markets cannot themselves cure unemployment and hence require extraordinary government intervention in order to avert free fall.[87]

It was not just Keynes who ignored Modigliani. So have contemporary Keynesians such as Paul Krugman, a particularly vigorous defender of central bank and other government interventions to turn around a weak economy. In 1994, Krugman wrote that

> to many people it seems obvious that massive economic slumps have deep roots. To them, [the argument] that they can be cured by [the government] printing a bit more money seems unbelievable.[88]

Note Krugman's choice of words: "a bit more money." After the unparalleled and truly massive money "printing" that followed the Crash of 2008, (the full size of which will be discussed in a later chapter), these words seem ridiculous, particularly since all the new money obviously failed to right the economy.

How did Krugman and Fed officials respond to the evident failure of their prescription? Chicago Fed bank president Charles Evans said that more had to be done. He did not want historians saying the Fed had not done enough. This was not unlike the philosophy that led George Washington's physicians to bleed him to death. Bleeding the patient was an accepted remedy at the time, and each physician, unwilling to do less than the other, kept bleeding until our founding father died.

Evans also stated that

> failure to act aggressively now will affect the capacity of the economy for years to come.

This is another old Keynesian chestnut. If the economy is sick, push the patient out of bed by whatever means, even if in the process you just make the malady worse. It is functionally equivalent to giving a drunk one last drink in the hope of steadying him.

16

How Dr. Fed Makes the Patient Sicker 2

KRUGMAN'S RESPONSE TO the failure of his own money printing recommendations after 2008 was not simply to call for more money printing. He also wanted to see more of the other Keynesian prescription, government deficit spending, which, as we have seen, is also largely financed by the Fed. Other Keynesians agreed.

Economists Brad DeLong and Lawrence Summers (the latter President Obama's first chief economic advisor) wrote a paper[89] in which they argued that more government deficit spending would both create jobs and reduce federal debt. This was yet another Keynesian paradox: more debt would not increase, but magically reduce, the total level of debt. This came from

Democrats who had previously derided the Republican idea that lowering taxes would magically increase revenue and thus also reduce government debt.

Proponents of more government debt of course rarely if ever call it debt. They call it "stimulus," or "investment," or simply "growth." Referring to borrowing as "growth" (as in we need more "growth") has been a favorite turn of phrase of President Obama, who borrowed it from President Hollande of France.

Keynesian economists recommending more money printing and government debt are almost as confusing and oracular as the politicians. Exactly how much "stimulus" do they want? How much growth or employment will it give us? They do not say. Keynes had said that increased deficit spending under such circumstances would pay for itself:

> Public works even of doubtful utility may pay for themselves over and over again at a time of severe unemployment, if only from the diminished cost of relief expenditure.[90]

He further elaborated by saying that for each dollar spent, there would be

at least three or four times

as many dollars of GDP growth and as many as twelve.

Where did these numbers come from? Apparently they came out of thin air. Keynes said at one point to Montague Norman, governor of the Bank of England, that his theories were a

> mathematical certainty, [not] open to dispute,[91]

but that was just a crude bluff.

Keynesian economists have never been able to document the returns Keynes promised from deficit spending. They have not even been able to demonstrate conclusively one dollar of GDP growth from a dollar borrowed and spent. As we have seen in Chapter 12, it should logically depend on the prior level of debt and also on how wisely the debt is used. Under the debt-choked circumstances of 2008–2009, it is likely that a dollar of deficit spending produced much less than a dollar of economic growth, and just added to the mass of debt to be repaid.

By 2012, four years after the Crash, some Keynesians were complaining that their pleas had been ignored, that the deficit spending following the Crash had not been of sufficient scale. But if you check what Keynesian economists Paul Krugman, Robert Shiller, and Christina Romer (chair of President Obama's Council of Economic Advisors) actually said after the Crash, it was never specific. Shiller said that stimulus

> has to be done on a big enough scale [and will be needed] for a long time in the future.[92]

Romer said:

> Beware of cutting back on stimulus too
> soon.[93]

How helpful! This was "heads I win, tails I win, too
advice." If the economy recovers, stimulus did it. If
not, there just was not enough stimulus. No matter
what happened, the Keynesians could claim that they
had been right. And their policy advice for the Fed
was equally free of specifics.

In addition to the usual government deficit spending that Keynes recommended, some economists,
including Paul Krugman, have argued for an alternative form of "stimulus" called "regulatory Keynesianism." The idea here is that government neither
borrows nor spends but rather requires businesses
to spend. For example, if environmental regulations
are tightened so that businesses must spend more to
comply, this is seen, not as a cost to the economy, but
as a job creator. When the Obama administration
decided not to tighten air pollution rules related to
ground level ozone, Krugman complained that

> tighter ozone regulation would actually have
> created jobs, forc[ing] firms to spend on
> upgrading or replacing equipment, helping
> to boost demand. Yes, it would have cost
> money—but that's the point.[94]

The underlying concept comes indirectly from Keynes, who wanted spending, no matter where the spending came from, and who joked that government should stimulate demand, and with it employment, by burying bank notes in old mines and inviting business firms to dig them up. At least in this fanciful suggestion, the businesses are given incentives, not legal requirements to spend or face fines or go to jail.

Thomas Geoghegan offered a further variant of the "stimulate no matter how" school in his Bloomberg article entitled "Obama Is Lucky that Medicare Is Out of Control." He writes that

> President Barrack Obama [can] thank his lucky stars that entitlements are out-of-control. . . . Out-of-control healthcare spending is the only stimulus the Republicans can't stop.[95]

Both regulatory Keynesianism and the related paradox of soaring medical costs "stimulating" the economy both share the same fallacy: that it does not really matter how we spend our money. What this fails to acknowledge is that we still live in a world of scarcity. Billions of people still lack the most basic necessities. If we waste resources, we cannot put them where they are really needed. As previously noted, what counts in spending, as in investment, is quality, not quantity, a theme which cannot be overemphasized, but which is missing entirely from most of contemporary economics.

In all these proposals for more spending, from whatever source, but especially from government borrowing, which in turn is supported by government printing of new money, used either to keep interest rates low or buy the government debt outright, we hear nice bedtime stories with happy endings. We do not hear any hard evidence in support of piling on more government money printing, debt, and spending sprees, because no such evidence exists. Nor do we hear logical arguments in support of it.

Robert Schiller, a leading Keynesian who teaches at Yale, begins an article this way:

> [A] fact . . . about our current economic situation . . . can no longer be denied: our economy is in desperate need of government stimulus.[96]

Does the rest of the article provide a defense of stimulus? No. Since the need for stimulus is undeniable, there is no need to defend it. Shiller apparently thinks that no reasonable person can disagree.

But reasonable people do disagree, strongly disagree. Robert Barro, the distinguished Harvard economist, wrote an article about the same time as Schiller's explaining why neither logic nor evidence supports government stimulus programs. Barro is far from alone, among either economists or the general public.

In fairness to Paul Krugman, the most famous current advocate of more Keynesian stimulus, he did not just call for the Fed to print more money and for the government to borrow and spend even larger amounts of money. He also proposed new labor rules that would make it more difficult for employers to fire anyone. As he said in November 2009:

> ... In normal times, there is something to
> be said for [allowing] employers [to] fire
> workers at will. ... But these aren't nor-
> mal times.[97]

It is worth taking a moment to consider just how reckless this proposal is. President Hoover intervened in the free price system after 1929 by cajoling employers not to reduce wages and threatening them if they did. As we have seen, this left employers facing bankruptcy with only one way to reduce labor costs, layoffs, and resulted in mass firings. In 2009, Krugman was intent on closing even this escape hatch of layoffs. If companies facing bankruptcy can neither reduce wages nor reduce staff, how can they survive? Indeed, how can the economy survive? Even in good times, companies forbidden to fire will be afraid to hire.

17

"First Do No Harm"

WHAT ARE THE alternatives to Krugman, who would not only run the printing presses and borrow, but would even bring government into every business hiring and firing decision? What should the government do in the face of an economic bust of its own making? The answer is simple: Remember the Hippocratic Oath for physicians: "First do no harm." Stop causing mayhem. Stop confusing, manipulating, and controlling prices. Allow free prices to do their work within the economy. Allow the patient to recover.

As this author wrote in another book:

> If an economy is stumbling, and unemployment is high, it means that some prices

are far out of balance with others. Wages, for example, may be too high in relation to prices, because prices have fallen at the onset of an economic slump. But if so, the problem is not all wages or all prices.

Some companies, some industries may be doing well; others may be in desperate straits. What is needed is an adjustment of particular wages and particular prices within and between companies, within and between industries, within and between sectors. These adjustments are not a one-time event. They must be ongoing, as each change leads to another in a vast feedback loop.

In some cases, the wages or other prices should rise. In other cases, they should fall. No single across-the-board adjustment will work. It will just make things worse. The economy is not a water tank to be filled or drained until the right level is reached. Such crude plumbing will not adjust or coordinate anything. It will just make a mess.[98]

A thriving economy is comprised of billions of prices and trillions of price relationships. Left alone, these prices almost miraculously coordinate demand with supply so that buyers obtain as much as possible of what they want. Refusing to let prices fall or pushing them higher (2% a year, per the Fed's target, linked to an artificial and dubious constructed index) is like jamming a stick into the spokes of a wheel or pouring sand into the fuel tank of an engine. If we do this, we should not wonder if the wheel ceases to turn or the engine refuses to run. Nor will other, equally grand "price rectification" schemes work any better.

John Maynard Keynes stated that uniform wage reductions would be a very useful tool to increase employment, if only they could be enforced.[99] Economist Ken Mayland echoed this in 2010 when he wrote an article entitled "To Create Jobs, Cut Everyone's Pay 10%."[100] But all of these grand schemes are misguided; they would just cause more trouble. It is not all wages or all prices that need adjustment. It is particular wages and prices. Left alone, the price system will sort it out, restore profitability, and, doing so, both restore and create jobs.

18

Facing Up to Past Mistakes

IN CHAPTER 7, we discussed how important loss and bankruptcy are for the free price system. The carrot of profit is a powerful motivator in persuading people to make necessary changes or at least to accept those changes. The fear of loss and bankruptcy is even more powerful.

Psychological studies have demonstrated that while people naturally want a financial gain, they especially want to avoid a loss. The fear of bankruptcy leads people to think through both risk and potential return carefully. If the threat of bankruptcy is removed, behavior will be much more reckless. This behavior will in turn lead to busts.

At the same time, bankruptcy serves a further purpose. It liquidates the errors of the past, and redirects salvageable assets to more competent hands. When mistakes are made, the price system, left to itself, both recognizes and corrects them. A foundation is thereby laid for future productivity and growth.

After the Japanese crash in the late 1980s, authorities refused to let this process proceed. As a result, what came to be called "zombie banks," only half alive, cluttered the financial system, along with "zombie companies" dependent on "zombie bank" credit lines. The resources that were poured into these banks and companies were not available for other, better uses, and the entire economy has remained in a comatose state ever since.

Acknowledgement of error, acceptance of loss, and even bankruptcy are hard disciplines. But they are inescapable in a healthy economy.

Why then does the US Fed constantly intervene to save banks and financial firms from their own mistakes? Why does it intervene to rescue the stock market? As we noted in the last chapter, Benjamin Strong of the New York Fed wrote in 1927 that he had intentionally given a

> coup de whiskey

to stock market prices,[101] a move that led directly to the Crash of 1929. Similarly, Fed Chairman Ben Bernanke patted himself on the back for the "coup de whiskey" he had given stocks post-crash in his 2010 *Washington*

Post article.[102] There is little or no empirical evidence
that supporting stock prices leads to more sustainable
employment or really helps the economy as a whole,
but none of that seemed to concern Bernanke. He had
begun a massive bail-out of financial firms and stock
prices in 2008 and continued with it long after the
Crash was over.

There is a good deal of debate about the size of
the Fed's Crash bailout, but "massive" is an accurate
adjective. Bernanke himself claimed that the Fed had
lent $1.2 trillion, representing about 9% of the econ-
omy's total annual output at the time and 38% of federal government spending. Many experts do not agree
with how the lending figure was calculated. And there
were also asset purchases and loan guarantees.

A study by economists at the University of Missouri-
Kansas City funded by the Ford Foundation puts the
total of all Fed commitments during the crisis at $29
trillion.[103] This $29 trillion was in addition to commit-
ments by the rest of the government which came to
as much as $17 trillion, although a smaller figure was
actually spent.[104] Nor did the engineering stop there.
After the Fed's balance sheet was increased $1.7 trillion
during the crisis, it was increased another $600 billion
through what came to be called "quantitative easing,"
a clunky euphemism for the government printing new
money, and another $700 billion by the end of 2012
with no end of the monetary expansion in view.

It is easy to miss the fine print in all of this, which often involves many billions. For example, when the Fed creates new money out of thin air by "buying" government bonds, it then books interest on those bonds. Some of this interest is used to pay Fed expenses, which are neither paid nor approved by Congress, and the rest is sent to the Treasury Department.

In 2012, this dividend sent to the Treasury amounted to $89 billion.[105] So in effect the government was not only selling bonds to itself. It was also relying on "income" from itself to reduce its budget deficit, which even after this trick was reported at about $1.2 trillion.

The $1.2 trillion figure was distorted in other ways as well. It was concocted by using accounting that would have sent any business executive to jail and in particular ignored growing liabilities in Medicare and Social Security. The real deficit based on generally accepted accounting practices (GAP) might easily have reached $7 trillion.[106]

Senator Dick Durban (D-Illinois) has tried to sidestep this issue by claiming that

> Social Security does not add a penny to our deficit.[107]

Note that he drops any reference to Medicare or Medicaid. And even then his assertion is only true if the federal government is prepared to renege on the entitlement commitments it has made.

If we include federal employee retirement commitments and entitlements, the total debt of the US is not the officially acknowledged $17.5 trillion, but rather something over $83 trillion.[108] That works out to almost $700,000 per taxpayer, and some analysts put the figure much higher, as high as $222 trillion.[109] These figures ought not only to give pause to taxpayers, but also to anyone thinking of investing in US government bonds, especially longer-term bonds. This may be why the Fed wants to be able to intervene and buy bonds whenever it chooses.

What all of this illuminates is that when the Fed bailed out Wall Street in 2008, it was also in effect bailing out the government, keeping the government debt machine running. What was in Bernanke's mind? We cannot of course say with certainty.

Protecting the government bond market would certainly have been a priority for him. In doing this, he must also have known that he was enabling profligate Washington spending that could not have taken place without his backing. He was himself the coiner of the term "fiscal cliff," which implicitly warned, in classic Keynesian terms, against cutting deficit spending too fast. And when Treasury Secretary Geithner in January 2013 proposed eliminating congressional approval of the federal debt ceiling, hitherto at least a cosmetic barrier to unlimited deficit spending, Bernanke told students at the University of Michigan in January 2013:

> I think it would be a good thing if we didn't
> have [it].[110]

When elected politicians decide to rescue private market participants, the motive is often quite transparent. For example, President Obama is thought to have intervened to save General Motors because auto workers predominate in the "swing" states most hotly contested by the two parties during presidential elections and because the United Auto Workers union is a key Democratic Party ally. The GM bailout is generally believed to have enabled President Obama to carry Ohio, the key swing state, in the 2012 election. The motives of the Bernanke Fed in bailing out Wall Street are undoubtedly more complicated.

Another factor to be considered, in addition to the desire to safeguard federal bond markets, is that the Fed system is itself at least in part run by Wall Street and regional financial firms, indeed was set up that way in 1913 when the underlying legislation passed. At the time of the 2008 Crash, a former head of Goldman Sachs was chairman of the New York Fed, another secretary of the Treasury, and there were many interlocking relationships. Fed staffers often hope to work in Wall Street and have an incentive to stay on good terms with their future employers. Moreover, these staffers can always tell themselves and others, as they hand out favors, that they are just following accepted Keynesian economic doctrines. Had not Keynes specifically stated that misdirected investment, as in a bubble, was better than no investment at all, that it is a "serious error" to regard bankruptcy or recession as necessary disciplines, and that policymakers should attempt to

abolish slumps

and seek to maintain a perpetual

quasi-boom?[111]

Keynesian economist Paul Krugman, like Keynes, does not think that a bubble is all bad. In 2002 he wrote in the *New York Times* that

Alan Greenspan needs to create a housing bubble to replace the Nasdaq bubble and [it appears] he . . . thinks he can pull that off,[112]

although he later reversed course and blamed Greenspan for ignoring

warnings about an emerging bubble.[113]

Krugman also ridiculed the idea that recessions are a

necessary punishment

for the errors of the bubble.[114]

This is, however, a mischaracterization of the position of free price proponents. They do not regard recession as either necessary or a punishment. They regard it as a recognition of reality, and also as a way of removing economic wreckage and debris so that the economy can resume its way forward.

Robert Solow is an especially respected Keynesian economist who taught at MIT and served in President Kennedy's Council of Economic Advisors. He wrote that

> [to say] a recession weeds out inefficient firms and practices . . . is a little like saying . . . a plague cleans up the gene pool.[115]

This is an extraordinarily misguided statement. In the first place, how can Wall Street firms, borrowing up to 30 times the value of their capital in order to speculate, confident that the Fed will rescue them if necessary, be compared to plague victims? Nor is it even accurate to say that recessions, absent government intervention, weed out such practices and firms. It is the firms' own actions which do the weeding.*

Economics is admittedly a confusing subject. A writer for the *New Yorker* magazine proclaimed in

---

* It is true that recessions may have millions of innocent victims, such as the low income people who bought houses at inflated prices during the 2000s housing bubble. But these people were lured into inappropriate debt by the Fed's own recklessness in fueling the bubble, along with other government policies subsidizing and promoting mortgage lending. And, when the music stopped, it was not the innocent victims who were bailed out. It was the big financial firms on Wall Street, and around the world.

September 2009 that Alan Greenspan and Ben Bernanke were Republicans who had followed a

> free-market [policy]

of keeping

> interest rates exceptionally low.[116]

How could the writer consider government price manipulation a free market policy? Presumably the reasoning was that Wall Street wanted low interest rates and Wall Street embodied free market thinking, although as we have seen, Wall Street has not the slightest interest in either free markets or free prices.

Even quite sophisticated minds may become confused about what is taking place before, during, and after a crash. *The Economist* magazine announced in an August 2010 editorial that

> this newspaper believes passionately in the principle of free markets. . . . But . . . asset markets do not work as well as those for consumer goods. . . . Central banks and governments do have to intervene when credit growth and asset prices (particularly in housing) start dancing their toxic two-step.[117]

Because *The Economist* fails to understand the central banks' role in obliterating free prices and blowing up the bubble in the first place, it inadvertently calls for central banks to do more of the same. In effect, the magazine, like George W. Bush[118] and other Keynesians, thinks that the best way to "save" the free price system is to "abandon" it. With friends like these, free prices do not need any enemies.

As the Fed massively intervenes to bail out Wall Street, a pertinent question is whether the agency might itself eventually require a bail-out. As of October 2011, the US Fed was leveraged 55:1 (debt-to-equity). The New York Fed was 105:1. What happens if there is a miscalculation and the Fed loses money? Not to worry. It does not even need to print money to cover the loss. It has decided on its own (release H.4.1 dated January 6, 2011) that any such losses will be borne by US taxpayers. Some central banks have even more leverage. The Chinese central banks debt-to-equity as of August 2011 was 1,286:1.[119]

19

Banking and Finance: The Great Fiction

I N THE 1930s, communism and fascism vied for world dominance. Under the former, government owned the economy. Under the latter, government controlled the economy, but did not directly own it.

The fascist system was really just a theatrical variant on the monarchical/mercantilist system that had prevailed for centuries in Europe, which had always possessed signal advantages for public officials. If the economy performs poorly, it can be blamed on markets or more tellingly on what President Theodore Roosevelt called "malefactors of great wealth." If the economy performs well, then government, or the government's central bank, can claim full credit.

The degree of government control under this kind of system varies. In the US, control of the banks, and increasingly the entire financial system, is tight. There are few, if any, free prices. The free price system has been replaced by a host of rules, subsidies, guarantees, and outright price controls.

The fiction is maintained that banking is part of a market system. But it is not. It is strictly a department of government. Moreover the rules that have been established for it make no sense, so it is forever in crisis. A department of government, it is also a ward of government.

This system can be very lucrative for public officials. Banks can be counted on to buy US government debt in massive quantities. Indeed that is currently their primary purpose. In addition, firms so completely dependent on Washington offer campaign contributions to elected officials and well-paid jobs to former officials and regulators. If regulations are violated, fines or court settlements can also be imposed, in addition to the usual taxes. These in effect become windfalls for the political system.

The wards do well too. They have first access to all the new money being printed by the Fed, and can either speculate with it or lend it on. Should securities market prices fall, or threaten to fall, the Fed will support them, as we have seen.

This might seem to be a golden arrangement, at least for the politicians and Wall Street bankers, but there is a flaw, even for them. As Ludwig von Mises explained, no economic system can expect to succeed without free prices. It may seem to succeed for a time, but will grow less and less stable, and eventually collapse, as the Soviet Union did.

Big banks may appear to be a wellspring of wealth, but the wellspring is prone to periodic crises. If the crisis is severe, bank shareholders and bondholders may forfeit the accumulated profits of decades, unless immediately rescued by government. Looked at over the long run, it is not clear that banks, as presently organized, earn any profits at all.

In 2008, the bank rescue took a great variety of forms. The government's original idea, embodied in the TARP legislation, was to buy the bad mortgages destroying bank solvency, but there was an immediate obstacle. Since the government had taken control of the mortgage market, there were no prices for the new bundled mortgage securities. It was not even possible to construct fictional prices; there was nowhere even to begin.

The lack of prices was compounded by a new regulatory requirement called, with unintended irony, "mark to market." Regulators intended that bank assets would reflect market prices, which would make it more apparent which banks were financially sound. But since there are no actual market prices in banking, this new rule created chaos. If one type of loan for $1,000 had been sold by a bank for $100, then all such loans were required to be marked down 90%, and on this basis very few banks could claim to be solvent.

A further complicating factor is that US banks are only required to hold a maximum 10% reserve against customer deposits. This assumed that depositors would never demand more than 10% of their funds back at any one time. If this calculation proved to be wrong, the bank would be unable to repay depositors as promised. Because of the 10% deposit requirement, known in the industry as a fractional reserve, banks are technically insolvent all the time. They are an accident waiting to happen.

Fractional reserve banking guarantees instability in the banking and financial sector and, ultimately, in the economy as a whole. But government favors it. Indeed, one of the first steps by the new Federal Reserve in 1914 was to reduce required bank reserves, and it has repeatedly reduced them since then. Why? Why does government reduce rather than increase required bank reserves, thereby making the system more unstable?

The short answer is that the government and the Fed think that lower reserves will stimulate more lending which will, at least in the short run, stimulate the economy. How does this work? For purposes of illustration, assume that person A deposits $1,000 in a bank. Person A expects to be able to withdraw the money anytime. But since the bank is only required to maintain a 10% reserve, it lends $900 to person B. Person B then deposits the $900 in another bank, also expecting to be able to draw it out anytime, but the second bank lends out $810 to person C. Person C also deposits in a third bank, which lends $729 to person D. And so on it goes until, under a 10% reserve system, up to $10,000 may have been borrowed.

This $10,000 is not new wealth; it has to be repaid. But it does represent new money, and all that new money should, in the short term, lead to additional economic spending. While this is happening, businesses and consumers will feel "good." But, if the process reverses, as it does in an economic downturn, if too many depositors want their money back or too many borrowers default, the collapse of all the credit and money piled up in what is really a legal "pyramid scheme" will not feel "good."

Economic thinker and writer Henry Hazlitt argued that the job of economists is to look past the seen to the unseen, past the near term to the long term. Politicians by contrast rarely look beyond the next election, and central bankers, appointed by the politicians, have not proved to be much different. This could not have been more apparent during the big bank mortgage crisis following the Crash of 2008. At that time, politicians and their appointees were thrashing about looking for quick fixes, and in the process further obliterating the free prices on which any successful economy depends.

Hank Paulson, Bush's Treasury secretary and former head of Goldman Sachs, itself bailed out by the government, had abandoned plans for the government to buy the bad bundled mortgages that no one could price. President Obama's incoming Treasury Secretary, Tim Geithner, in the spring of 2009 devised his own plan for dealing with the bad mortgages and thus rescuing the big banks. His scheme, called the Public-Private Partnership Investment Program, would have had government lend funds to Wall Street firms at minimal interest rates to buy the bad mortgages. The loans would have been secured only by the mortgages themselves, thus repayable only if the mortgages were repaid.

Even this virtual gift of government money to already rich investors failed. It did not address, indeed it just further complicated, the underlying problem, which was the impossibility of buying or selling the bundled mortgages without any idea what they were worth. This was information only free prices could provide.

By August 2010, Bill Gross, chief executive of the largest bond manager in the US, Pacific Investment Management, was calling for complete nationalization of mortgage finance.[120] But the Fed was busy with its more subtle solutions, whose implications were understood by few. It held short-term interest rates below the rate of inflation, so the banks could borrow at virtually no cost. It used newly created money to buy longer US or US agency bonds, which made the bonds owned by the banks rise in value. By promising to keep short rates close to zero for a long time, it encouraged banks and other Wall Street firms to borrow vast sums for short periods, while lending to the government at much higher rates for longer periods, thus guaranteeing big profits.

Investment banks such as Goldman Sachs, speculators par excellence, were also recategorized as deposit-taking banks. This major departure from the past meant that they were now eligible to receive directly the Fed's giveaway money. David Stockman, Budget Director under President Reagan referred to this decision as

a Robin Hood redistribution in reverse.[121]

At each step of the way, the Fed was further obscuring price information. For example, before 2008, investors could compare yields of straight Treasury bonds to those of the Treasury's consumer-price-inflation-adjusted bonds. The difference was thought to represent inflation expectations. Once the Fed started buying all these securities, in unknown amounts, this useful information disappeared. The Fed also contributed its share of the estimated 14,125 new bank policy and regulatory changes issued by governments worldwide in the year immediately following the Crash. 57% originated in North America according to Thomson Reuters.[122]

Not to be outdone in regulatory zeal, the US Congress in 2010 passed the 2,323-page Dodd-Frank Wall Street Reform and Consumer Protection Act, which in turn required the further drafting of 400 new rules.[123] Six months later, only 21 of the 400 had been drafted in preliminary form, and it was thought that the completion of the regulations would require several hundred thousand pages and up to five years. Economist Steve Hanke responded that it would have been more realistic to create just a few simple, transparent, and enforceable rules such as an increased reserve ratio, and leave it at that.[124]

The Dodd-Frank Act also created the Consumer Financial Protection Bureau, which it placed inside the Fed, where as we have noted, it could be funded outside the congressional budgeting process and therefore without increasing the government deficit. Newly hired staffers lost no time in getting down to the question of how

> to verify a borrower's ability to repay a mortgage,

as reported by the *American Banker*.[125] Apparently this responsibility had now been assumed by the government, since "too big to fail" banks could no longer be relied on to do their own banking.

By the end of 2012, it was discovered that some banks were simply making up the Libor interest rate (London Interbank Offered Rate) which is often used as a basis for other rates, including mortgage rates. This was supposed to be shocking and unacceptable. But the truth is that almost nothing in banking today is real anymore. It long ago lost any solid connection to market reality and is all fictional to one degree or another.

20

Baby Steps in the Right Direction

EDGING EVER CLOSER to de facto national-ization of the banks, while maintaining the pretense that they are still part of a free price market system, does not accomplish anything. It just makes the banking system even more unstable, which will plunge the economy into even deeper miseries. So what would help?

Sheila Baer, former chairman of the Federal Deposit Insurance Corp., and a lonely voice of sanity during and after the 2008 Crash, offers a tongue-in-cheek solution in a *Washington Post* article.[126] Why not, she says, expand the Fed's current welfare system for banks, financial firms, and wealthy investors to everyone else? Why not, in short, print sufficient new money to lend every US household $10 million at zero interest rates?

In this case, suggests Ms. Baer, each household would be able to emulate the banks and reinvest the $10 million in 10-year government bonds yielding a projected 2%, thereby generating $200,000 in annual income. The more adventurous could even reinvest in Greek debt paying 21% at the time, thereby earning $2.1 million a year. With all that income, everyone could simply pay off those bad mortgages and any other bad debts.

In one stroke, the banking system regains its feet—and the economy revives with massive Keynesian "demand" from new consumer purchases. Best of all, the government can put an end to its deficit spending because of a gusher of taxes on the new interest income. All the government has to do to get this ball rolling is to treat all of us like banks and hedge funds by printing up $1.2 trillion dollars, or $10 million for each of 120 million households.

Sheila Baer remains tongue-in-cheek, but we will fess up that none of this will work. If the Fed did it, everyone's income would soar, and so would consumer demand. Unfortunately, the supply of goods and services would remain unchanged, or more likely collapse, because so many people would quit their jobs. With demand soaring and supply shrinking, the price of available goods and services would also soar. In short order, we would find that our fabulous new incomes would not actually buy anything more than our old incomes did.

Unfortunately printing money cannot create real wealth. Saving, sound investment, and hard work are all needed for that. The only way to make money from money printing is to get the new money first, before others do, which is how banks and financial firms get rich off of it, at least for a time.

Sheila Baer's parable is a useful reminder of reality, but what serious bank reform proposals might make sense? A common suggestion is to revive the Depression era Glass-Steagall Act. Until repeal in 1999, this forbade deposit-taking banks from investment banking, trading, and generally from competing with Wall Street speculators, which was intended to keep federally guaranteed institutions out of trouble.

The usual explanation for repeal is that the old safeguards were not needed anymore and the banks were being hamstrung. Dennis K. Berman offered another rationale in the *Wall Street Journal*:

> [The] theory [in repealing Glass-Steagall is that] putting... more speculative realms of investment banking and trading [inside] a large, plodding typical bank—with stable deposits and returns—... solves ... problems.[127]

During and after the Crash, financial regulators embraced this theory with gusto, most dramatically forcing Bank of America to absorb the failing investment banker and broker Merrill Lynch. The logic behind this was exceptionally poor. Deposit-taking banks, with their pyramids of loans, were anything but "stable." To force mergers with investment bankers, brokers, and traders simply poured gasoline on the fire.

At the same time, movement in the opposite direction—reinstating a legal separation of activities as in Glass-Steagall, also poses risks. Much has happened since the 1930s. Large corporations depend much less on ordinary bank loans than in the past. This is one reason why a failure of large banks in 2008 would not have led to a cascade of corporate failures. But if contemporary banks, which have lost so many major corporate customers, are suddenly limited by law to old-fashioned lending, they might turn out to be unprofitable, not just in the long run, taking into account the devastation of crashes, but even in the short run.

If this happened, if banks could no longer even pretend to be profitable, these wards of government and indispensable tools of government finance would no doubt be propped up forever by state subsidies. It would be as if, when autos first appeared, the government had decided to keep buggy and buggy whip manufacturers going forever regardless of demand. The crucial difference is that the buggy manufacturers were not primary buyers of government bonds—and banks are.

During the first nine months of 2009, in the teeth of the financial crisis, banks in Britain and the US each bought about $240 billion of government debt. By doing so, they, helped preserve the credit standing of their rescuers.[128] It is very unlikely that these same governments would ever let them disappear, especially since it is so much easier to disguise subsidies to banks than subsidies to buggy manufacturers.

Reviving Glass-Steagall prohibitions is better than nothing. But it is not a solution. There really is no solution for the lending industry so long as it remains tightly controlled by government, effectively if not explicitly nationalized, relying on phony prices, and run for the benefit of government and its private cronies on Wall Street. A more root and branch reform is needed, beginning with elimination of fractional reserve banking, and concluding with the creation of a new monetary system.

21

Real Banking Reform

THE ELIMINATION OF fractional reserve banking is not a new idea. An effort to require banks to maintain a 100% reserve narrowly failed in English courts in 1811 and 1816 and again in the House of Lords in 1848.[129] The moral and legal argument was sound, that banks promising to repay depositors on demand while lending the money elsewhere were committing a fraud.

The economic argument against fractional reserve banking, also dating to the 19th century, was equally sound. It held that pyramiding loans, in the process flooding an economy with new money, was bound to cause instability. Far better for banks to take deposits and act as agents for the depositors rather than principals. If I, a depositor, want to earn interest, the bank could arrange a loan and take a fee for doing so. I would agree to give up any right to withdraw my money during the term of the loan.

Under this arrangement, there could be no "runs" on a bank in which fearful depositors want all their money bank at once, so government deposit insurance would no longer be necessary. With deposit insurance gone, it would then become possible to eliminate government's control of everyday banking operations. Banks would still of course operate under the common law, which would require compliance with depositor contracts and forbid any fraudulent activity. Banking would not be lawless; it would operate like any other business within a framework of laws applicable to everyone.

Proposals to increase bank reserves are common. For example, Alan Meltzer, distinguished historian of the Fed, has suggested an increase from 10% to 20%.[130] It has also been noted, after 2008, that the Canadian banking system, which had higher reserve requirements, fared better.[131] Ken Rogoff, professor of economics at Harvard, stated a year after the Crash that

> the banks ... ought to have a lot of cash on hand in reserve [to backstop short-term borrowing] and the system doesn't require it.[132]

Although most such proposals want to tinker with fractional reserves, not eliminate the concept entirely, arguments for 100% reserves have been made over the years. Proponents have included such eminent economists as Frank Knight and Henry Simons of the University of Chicago, Irving Fisher of Yale, and in particular "Austrian" school economists led by Ludwig von Mises. Keynesian economists mostly ignore all this. For example, Keynesian economist Paul McCulley penned the following remarkable lines on November 2008, in the midst of the Crash:

> Yes, sometimes we collectively end up paying $800 for military toilet seats, as was the case about 25 years ago [when the Defense Department bought them]. But that doesn't change the proposition that public goods do exist, and a stable system of intermediation of private savings into private investment is indeed a public good. The maturity transformation power of a fractional reserve banking system provides an unambiguous benefit to society and as such, must be underwritten by society.[133]

When McCulley speaks (in financial jargon) of the "maturity transformation power of . . . fractional reserve[s]," he is presumably describing how the system takes a short-term deposit, due back to the depositor on demand, and turns it into an illiquid loan, not at all returnable on demand. This is hardly an

unambiguous benefit.

It is instead a mismatch of depositor and borrower that contributes to instability and crashes.

It is worth noting that McCulley, like most contemporary Keynesians, does not bother to support or even argue his position. For him, Keynesian ideas are a kind of received truth, beyond any need for review or discussion. Fed Chairman Ben Bernanke adopted a similar position when questioned in House Banking Committee meetings 2010–2012 by Chairman Ron Paul. He barely suppressed a half smile or smirk when answering, as if criticisms of Keynesian beliefs were inane.

The truth about fractional reserve banking was summed up by Martin Wolf, the distinguished former World Bank economist and columnist for the *Financial Times*:

> There is [a] way of making finance safe. . . .
> It [is] radical: deposits would be 100% reserve backed. . . .

22

A New Monetary System

I F WE REALLY want to reform banking and finance, the source of so much instability and economic pain, elimination of fractional reserves will go far, but not far enough. So long as government controls money, it will also want to control banks, and it will use its control over both money and banking to finance itself in ways that distort free prices and lead to bubbles and busts. As noted in Chapter 11, bubbles and busts predated the modern banking system, although the Fed's reduction of fractional reserves has magnified them. Swiss economist Peter Bernholz notes that of the twenty-nine hyperinflations followed by bust in history he has been able to study, all but one took place after 1914, the beginning of the US Fed and the modern era of central banking.[134]

Even if the only money in the world were gold, and government had no control over it, there could still be a limited degree of bubble and bust activity. People in country A might borrow gold from country B, hoping to finance an exciting new industry and make fortunes from it. This could create unrealistic expectations, borrowing, and spending in country A, but the flow of money out of country B would reduce spending there, so the faster activity in one country would be offset by the slower activity elsewhere. Under these circumstances, a global crash such as in 2008 would be unimaginable. The bubble preceding that Crash was blown up with unlimited government money printing, and the Crash that followed led to even more promiscuous money printing, the wages of which have yet to be fully paid.

There are those few who, looking at government's willingness, indeed eagerness, to debase its own currency, call for a return to the global gold standard. When one hears this, one must ask: which gold standard? The one in the US that came into being in 1879 and ended with the creation of the Fed and World War I worked rather well, because politicians wishing to subvert it did not get into power. When they did, it disappeared, and the gold standards that followed were gold standards in name only.*

---

* See Hunter Lewis, *Are the Rich Necessary? Great Economic Arguments and How They Reflect Our Personal Values* (Mt. Jackson, VA: Axios Press, 2009), 321–38.

The problem with any global gold standard is that governments will control it. Eventually they will want more money than taxes provide, and the temptation to do whatever is necessary to get more of it will become too strong to resist. The only real solution is to remove the government, including the Fed, not only from the banking business, but from the money/currency/legal tender business.

Ludwig von Mises Institute chairman Llewellyn Rockwell explains:

> The 14th century Bishop Nicholas Oresme [wrote] as follows:
>
>> I am of the opinion that the main and final cause of why the prince pretends the power of altering the coinage is that profit or gain which he can get from it. . . . The amount of the prince's profits is necessarily that of the community's loss.[135]
>
> The techniques are different today, but the incentives and moral results are the same. [Guido] Hülsmann points to another change: today's princes have received absolution from the scientific authorities of our day. Princes used to work in secret to do these things, and be disgraced when caught. Now they announce the policy as

responsible statecraft that is consistent with the teaching of modern economics—and the economists stand ready to nod their heads in agreement. . . .

We will look back on the end of the Bush administration as an economic disaster, a capstone of many years of [errors]. They will be disgraced, as will the new administration that pursued all the wrong policy measures as a response. . . . In the face of this, it is time to deal with [a] political reality that no one in Washington (except Congressman Ron Paul) is even slightly interested in: an orderly plan to restore sound money. . . .

In an essay written at the end of his career, and recently brought back to life by the Mises Institute, [economist] F. A. Hayek discusses the only serious means of reform that is open to us. We must completely abolish the central bank. Money itself must be wholly untied from the state. It must be restored as a private good, privately produced for private markets. Government must have no role at all in monetary affairs. Money should be produced by private enterprise alone. Banks must exist only as free-enterprise institutions, with no privileges from the state. This plan has also been advanced by [Guido Hülsmann and Congressman] Ron Paul. ...

What is further striking about the Hayek, Hülsmann, and Paul idea here is that they offer no plan for restoring a gold dollar. It's not that they would disagree with the idea, but they have fully confronted the reality that the idea of converting the existing currency from fiat money to sound money is essentially a 19th century ideal that presupposes an enlightened class of political managers. This condition is not met today.

But what [then] is the means? It is the same with monetary policy and banking policy. ... Let failing banks die. Let profitable banks live. Let the people choose to use any form of money. Let the people choose any means of payment. Let entrepreneurs create any form of financial instrument. Law applies only the way it applies to all other human affairs: punishing force and fraud. Otherwise, the law should have nothing to do with it.

What would be the results? We cannot know for sure. But history can be a guide in our speculations. Throughout all time and in all places, precious metals have emerged as the foundation of the monetary system. I think we can have every expectation that the same would be true today. Evidence comes from how people turn to gold in difficult times as a store of value, a safe-house from the machinations of government. Gold, in my view, is destined to be the foundation of a new free-market monetary system. It will be the de facto result of having no monetary policy at all. A free market in money would work the same as a free market in everything else.

And consider: We are not asking Congress to intervene with a plan. No one is demanding that the Fed adopt this policy versus that policy. All we are asking is that it not intervene in the attempts by the market to fix the problems that have been created by the central bank and the executive department.

Just imagine what would happen if legal-tender laws were repealed and the government stopped intervention in the market for money. Virtually overnight, we would see the appearance of hundreds if not thousands of new payment systems and alternative monies online. Merchants would be free to accept any means of payment. There would be intense competition among them. Some would be foreign currencies like the Euro. Some would be new currencies based on existing commodities such as gold and silver. I'm certain that we would see a period of wild experimentation take place before the market settled back down again into a standard system that was famed for its reliability and stability and honesty.

Would we be able to endure the process of discovery? Certainly. We do this every day with our shopping online, or searches for good providers of services and products in the physical world, and our habits on how to invest our money.

The market is a process of trial and error, one that never stops innovating and changing. We see every day on the World Wide Web how this process of creation and change creates the right balance between chaos and order, experimentation and standardization. This would happen in the field of money too."[136]

23

Returning to America's Monetary Roots

OCKWELL'S PROPOSAL IS not as radical as it sounds. The government of Singapore already allows checking accounts and debit cards denominated in gold and silver.[137] In many respects, the proposal merely returns us to America's roots. The drafters of the US Constitution, intent on keeping power over money out of the hands of state governments, unwisely put it into the hands of the federal government. But they would have been appalled with what the federal government, and especially its agent the Federal Reserve, has done with that power.

Consider, for example, what the chief framer of the US Constitution, James Madison, had to say in 1786 about government-issued paper money:

> Paper money . . . is pernicious, destroying
> confidence between individuals; discour-
> aging commerce; enriching sharpers; viti-
> ating morals; reversing the end of govern-
> ment; and conspiring with the examples of
> other states to disgrace republican govern-
> ments in the eyes of mankind.[138]

Even Alexander Hamilton, another principal author of the Constitution and usually considered friendly to the idea of a larger role for government in the economy, expressly condemned the idea of allowing government to issue paper money:

> The emitting of paper money by the au-
> thority of Government is wisely prohib-
> ited. . . . Though paper emissions, under a
> general authority, might have some advan-
> tage . . . yet they are of a nature so liable
> to abuse—and it may even be affirmed,
> so certain of being abused—that the wis-
> dom of the Government will be shown in
> never trusting itself with the use of so se-
> ducing and dangerous an expedient. . . .
> The stamping of paper is an operation
> so much easier than the laying of taxes,
> that a government, in the practice of pa-
> per emissions, would rarely fail . . . to in-
> dulge itself too far in the employment of

> that resource . . . even to [the point of creating] an absolute bubble.[139]

Yes, Hamilton used the word "bubble" in expressing what he feared from paper money. In so doing, he presciently put his finger on the dilemma that the world economy faces today, as it struggles against the bubble and bust syndrome created by central bankers' unlimited creation of new money, most of which now takes electronic rather than paper form. It is of course even easier to "emit" electronic money than paper money, and far, far easier than raising taxes.

We should note, however, that Hamilton had no objection to private banks issuing notes that were the equivalent of paper money. That was different, because unlike government paper money, it could be regulated by market forces. If a private bank issued too much,

> it will return upon the bank,[140]

by which Hamilton meant that people would demand gold for the notes. A bank could be put out of business if everyone did this at once, so would take care to avoid it, even if fractional reserves were allowed.

It is commonly thought that Hamilton's opponent Thomas Jefferson and Jefferson's philosophical heir Andrew Jackson opposed banks. They did not. What they feared, and with good reason, was that central banks would become the tools of politicians and their rich supporters. As Jackson said:

> The mischief [in a central bank] springs from the power which the moneyed interest derives from a paper currency which they are able to control.[141]

One of the original supporters of the Federal Reserve Act of 1913, Senator Elihu Root, thought to include a provision barring government issued paper money. Then he reconsidered. It would surely be unnecessary, he thought, since any paper money issued would be backed by gold. How shocked he would be if could return today, to witness not only paper and electronic money backed by nothing, but every conceivable manipulation of it by the Fed.

24

Who Should Run the Economy?

I N CHAPTER 22, Llewellyn Rockwell suggested that "we the people" should run the money system through our own consumer choices. Money is a product, like any other, and a government monopoly of it just produces corruption, debased money, and irreparable injury to the free price system.

The counter-argument, that government knows best, is thousands of years old. Ancient Chinese annals tell us that the Han Dynasty emperor Wu-di (155–87 BCE) decided that government must control the economy, and castrated his advisor Sima Qian for daring to dispute his view. Although Wu-di said that he was setting up monopolies granted by the state in salt, iron, and other basic commodities in order to protect the common people from greedy merchants, his monopolies really just made a few merchants colossally rich, and ensured a steady stream of kickbacks from them to court officials and to the Emperor himself.

In similar fashion, the middle and later Roman emperors granted monopolies, instituted price controls punishable by death, debased the currency by stripping precious metals from coins, exacted ever harsher taxation, and reaped a whirlwind of corruption and economic collapse. As economist Jesus Huerta de Soto has written:

> Roman civilization did not fall as a result of the barbarian invasions.

It undermined itself from within through its own economic policies, although serious plagues also played a part in decimating and demoralizing the population.[142]

Economist John Maynard Keynes updated Wu-di and the Roman emperors by suggesting that the 20th century state would decide economic issues based on

> long views, . . . the . . . general social advantage[,] and . . . collective wisdom.[143]

He concluded that

> state planning, . . . intelligence and deliberation at the center must supersede the . . . disorder [of the past].[144]

It is notable that Keynes was not entirely consistent about this advice. He insisted that the future was unknowable, but seemed to forget this when extolling the "long views" of state planners. He also acknowledged the "muddle" that poor state policy choices had on occasion produced,[145] and even at one point referred to politicians as "utter boobies," thereby anticipating humorist P. J. O'Rourke's remark that

> bringing the government in to run Wall Street is like saying, "Dad burned dinner, let's get the dog to cook."[146]

It is likely that Keynes did not exactly mean what he said. He was not espousing economic leadership by elected officials. He acknowledged that they were chosen by

> the vast mass of more or less [economically] illiterate voters,[147]

and might be equally "illiterate." What he really wanted was control by state appointed experts, especially one expert—himself.

Other experts might do in a pinch, but Keynes further admitted that

> some of those representing themselves as such seem to me to talk much greater rubbish than an ordinary man could ever be capable of.[148]

Experts might talk "rubbish"; they might give way to emotion; they might even prove to be dishonest. Keynes acknowledged this. But it did not prevent him from wanting to put the control of all money under a single world organization, run by experts from different countries, which he insisted would offer:

> Plenary wisdom [and] scientific management.[149]

The collapse of the Soviet Union put some tarnish on Keynes's dream of economic control from "the center." The Soviet planners were not Keynesians; they were communists. But they were experts who had failed to show that experts could run an economy. In 1989, economist Robert Heibroner, a Keynesian and long-time proponent of planning, seemed ready to throw in the towel:

> The contest between capitalism and so-
> cialism is over: capitalism has won. [We
> now have] the clearest possible proof that
> capitalism organizes the material affairs
> of human-kind more satisfactorily than
> socialism.[150]

By 1997, *The Economist* magazine concluded that

> almost any discussion of public policy now-
> adays seems to begin and end with the same
> idea: the state is in retreat.[151]

To which Harvard economic historian David Landes added:

> [All] sides blithely assume that free markets
> are in the saddle and riding the world.[152]

But had the free price system really convinced its critics or emerged with new authority? If so, why was Europe embarking on its experiment of more and more central economic control, not only in monetary and cross border trade affairs, but in the most minute regulation of every aspect of economic life? Why were the Japanese centralizing their economy in response to their bubble and crash? Why were the Fed and other central banks around the world steadily tightening their grip on interest rates, currency, and money in general, thereby blowing up further bubbles that would inevitably lead to crashes? As economic writer James Grant noted:

> Central planning may be discredited in the
> broader sense, but people still believe in
> central planning as it is practiced by [The
> US Federal Reserve]. . . . To my mind the
> Fed is a cross between the late, unlamented
> Interstate Commerce Commission and the
> Wizard of Oz. It is a Progressive Era regulatory body that, uniquely among the institutions of that era, still stands with its
> aura and prestige intact.[153]

Economist William Anderson was even more critical:

> Central banking, for all its "aura," is no less socialistic than the Soviet Union's Gosplan [the Soviet agency charged with creating Communist Russia's economic plan].[154]

Like the Soviet Politburo and Gosplan, the Fed mostly works in secrecy. Minutes of board votes are eventually disclosed. But the way decisions are implemented is never revealed, and chairman Bernanke has denounced Congressman Ron Paul's call for congressional audits.

Although as much as possible is done behind a veil, there is really no mystery about the tools the Agency uses to reach decisions that will affect everyone. What is most notable about these tools is how few and how flimsy they are. There is much data collection. There are some models, respected by no one. As the Soviets discovered, models cannot take the place of a free price system. The models generate forecasts. Some of these have been published, and shown to be largely wrong.[155]

Chairman Ben Bernanke's own implicit forecasts have been startlingly wrong. He told Congress on February 15, 2006:

> Our expectation is that . . . house prices will probably continue to rise.

The subsequent crash brought them down by a national average of 31%. Again before Congress on March 28, 2007, he testified that

> . . . the impact on the broader economy and financial markets of the problems in the subprime [mortgage] market seems likely to be contained,

another spectacular error. At a luncheon in Washington on January 10, 2008, already one month into what became known as the Great Recession, he added that

> the Federal Reserve is not currently forecasting a recession.[156]

Even as late as July 2008, he insisted that mortgage giants Fannie Mae and Freddie Mac, already on the verge of collapse, were

> adequately capitalized [and] in no danger of failing.[157]

British statesman William Churchill quipped that

> a politician needs the ability to foretell what is going to happen tomorrow, next week, next month, and next year. And to have the ability afterward to explain why it didn't happen.[158]

By this standard, Bernanke and other Fed officials may not be good economists, but they are first rate politicians.

Fed chairmen Alan Greenspan and Ben Bernanke, Republicans who were reappointed by Democratic Presidents, both rejected calls for the Fed to follow some kind of formula or at least to operate from a rule. They insisted on what might be called a "seat of the pants" approach to Fed decision-making, and between the two of them, blew up enormous bubbles that brought the Crash of 2008.

The most celebrated rules designed to guide monetary policy were devised by economist Milton Friedman. But they depend on quantifying the money supply, and in today's complicated financial world, it is almost impossible to define money, much less quantify it. For example, nobody thought that homes were money, until home equity loans were invented and placed atop regular mortgages. At that point, a home became a source of ready cash for even ephemeral purchases.

A widely respected rule for setting the Fed Funds short-term interest rate was developed by economist John Taylor of Stanford. This rule might have avoided the bubbles and crashes of the 1990s and 2000s, but utilizes variables (potential output, inflation rate) that are difficult to define or observe and thus lead to debate and disagreement.[159] For example, in 2009 economists using the Taylor framework argued for a Fed Funds Rate ranging from the Fed's actual target of .25% to -5.8%. Taylor himself objected that those arguing for a policy of increasing inflation and simultaneously holding interest rates down to produce negative rates were not using his rule as intended.[160]

John Taylor would be an excellent Fed chairman, far better than any we have had since Paul Volcker. But is this really any way to run an economy? Should we be betting our future on failed forecasts, flawed models, and Talmudic discussions about what numbers to plug into them?

25

Last Stand of the Wizard of Oz

B Y THE END of 2012, the ad hoc policymaking of Chairman Ben Bernanke seemed to have painted the Fed into a corner. As the agency created almost three trillion of new money, it kept affirming that it could reverse course at any time and "drain" the new money out if unemployment fell back to 6.5% or consumer price inflation exceeded 2.5% according to its own measurements. But could the Fed do this? Could it actually reverse course?

To do so would mean selling the new trillions of debt to other parties. Who would these other parties be? Who could absorb so much debt in an already debt choked world? A highly respected analyst cal-culated that just raising interest rates to a relatively modest level of 2% would require cutting the present Fed balance sheet by over half. He likened the present Fed policy to the "roach motels" sold in hardware stores: easy to get into but impossible to exit.[161]

Whatever their eventual results, Bernanke's policies in 2012 seemed already to be failing, even when looked at in strictly Keynesian terms. As is the case with most economic "plans" concocted in an ivory tower, there had been "unintended consequences." For one thing, the forced reduction of interest rates to the vanishing point had not produced what the Keynesians most want: increased demand. One problem was that consumers had lost the interest income on savings that they otherwise would have had.

Yes, consumers also paid less on some of their own borrowing. But economist Randall Wray, not generally an anti-Keynesian, estimates that the loss of interest income was $200 billion a year more than the reduction in loan cost.[162] This meant that, even looking through a Keynesian lens, the Fed's actions in reducing interest rates "de-stimulated" rather than "stimulated" the economy.

Nor is this all. As Stanford economist Ronald McKinnon has pointed out, mindlessly promising to keep interest rates negligible for years, as the Fed did, discouraged potential borrowers from acting immediately to take advantage of low rates.[163] It also discouraged banks from lending, since the rates they would get were low, and they could earn profits just by borrowing themselves in the money market and using the proceeds to buy government bonds. We have already noted that getting banks to buy government bonds may have been exactly what Bernanke wanted, because he was really most worried about preserving the credit status of the US government. But, whatever the motive, his actions could not be shown to help reduce unemployment.

In general, the Fed's actions seemed tilted to favor the largest banks over the smaller ones, the ones more likely to lend to Main Street businesses. Thanks to the Fed, the six largest bank holding companies earned an aggregate $51 billion in 2009, the year following the Crash.[164] Competition had been reduced as smaller rivals failed. And both Fed largesse and the "too big to fail" doctrine reduced the behemoth's lending costs significantly below their remaining competitors.

During the same year, 2009, the 980 banks ranked in size after the top six lost money in aggregate.[165] Many of these banks remain in a slow motion death spiral. It is thought that compliance with the new Dodd-Frank law will be so expensive that many of them will be forced to merge or go out of business. But that will not be clear for many years. So in the meantime they hang on, not profitable, and hesitant to lend.

Professor McKinnon also points to another unintended consequence of the Fed's giveaway interest rates. They threatened defined benefit pension funds, which need to earn a minimum fixed income return in order to cover pension liabilities. It might be added that a similar problem affects insurance companies, which have been pushed into riskier investments in order to meet their minimum yield requirements. Will collapsing pension funds and insurance companies really improve the financial health of the US?

Repressed interest rates not only reduced demand, reduced bank lending, and threatened pension and insurance funds. The availability of cheap money also encouraged companies to replace labor, especially unskilled labor, with cheaply financed equipment, which reduced employment at just the wrong time. It was even more tempting for businesses to use the cheap money to buy other businesses, or just buy in their stock, rather than take a risk on new employees or equipment or especially to embark on new business ventures, the source of most new employment.

These are all what might be described as technical objections, on Keynesian grounds, to what Bernanke has done. But there is another major objection as well. Keynes was a great believer in what he called "animal spirits." He thought that if confidence was high, businesses and consumers would spend and invest and the economy would boom. By taking such extreme measures, Professor Bernanke has in all likelihood frightened the very people he wants to lend, spend, or invest.

Lenders are reluctant to lend because they worry that the Fed may create uncontrollable inflation and cause the value of their loan to plummet. Or they are just waiting, hoping that rates will finally be allowed to rise. Borrowers are afraid to borrow because they fear that they might not be able to refinance when their loans come due. Academics refer to this as an increase in the expected volatility of interest rates caused by the Fed's attempts to reduce volatility by artificial means.

Consumers are made uneasy in general as they hear about the extreme lengths to which the Fed is going. They also have to pay more for food and energy, prices that are not counted by the Fed in its inflation figures, but which are nevertheless driven up by Fed money creation. In this way, by creating more uncertainty rather than less, the Fed in effect becomes its own worst enemy.

The fundamental problem with Bernanke is not of course that he has applied Keynesianism incorrectly. Keynesianism itself is irredeemably flawed and would better be tossed onto the dustbin of history. But it is worth noting that even his supposedly Keynesian policy is loaded with self-contradictions.

Meanwhile the Fed seems in a state of complete denial. Chairman Bernanke has repeatedly denied that Fed policies brought on the housing bubble:

> The evidence that I've seen and that we've done within the Fed suggests that monetary

> policy did not play an important role in
> raising house prices during the upswing.[166]

Contrary to this remarkable statement, the evidence remains overwhelming that the Fed is directly responsible for the housing bubble, principally because of the giveaway interest rates that it engineered, but also because of a lack of regulatory oversight that at times tipped over into directly encouraging marginal loans. If Bernanke's present policy gambles continue to backfire, he will no doubt have an explanation for why the Fed should not be blamed.

The Federal Reserve has always been skilled at this kind of political obfuscation and "spin." Economist Milton Friedman noted in 1981, long before the advent of today's hyperactive central banks, that

> [the Federal Reserve] System ... blames all
> problems on external influences beyond
> its control and takes credit for any and
> all favorable occurrences. It thereby con-
> tinues to promote the myth that the pri-
> vate economy is unstable, while its behav-
> ior continues to document the reality that
> government is today the major source of
> economic instability.[167]

Following the Crash of 2008 and its aftermath, the Fed's myth-making is wearing thin. Many questions have been raised. Support is no longer unanimous among economists and public officials, although the public remains largely unaware of the debate. Economist Marc Faber predicted both the Crash and the Fed's sagging prestige. It is worth noting where he thought it would lead:

> If monetary policies and central-bank interventions in the market economy should now fail—as I believe they will—the economic textbooks of the post Second World War period...will have to be rewritten. I would also expect the power of central banks to be significantly curtailed.... When...the public...finally realizes that central bankers are no wiser than the central planners of former communist regimes, the tide will turn and monetary reform will come to the fore.... At that time ... market forces [will again] drive economic activity, and not some kind of central planner: regardless whether they stand forth as senior officials of totalitarian regimes—or come cleverly disguised as central bankers.[168]

26

Is the Fed's Behavior Moral?

I N AN EARLIER book, this author wrote:

Economist John Maynard Keynes spent most of his lifetime mocking the values of ordinary, middle-class people. It is not surprising that his economic theories, the theories that underlie modern central banking, turn the old copybook maxims of morality on their head. In the Keynesian world, technical cleverness matters more than hard work, spending is a virtue, saving is almost an antisocial act. People will be willful, capricious, subject to emotional extremes. But a wise government, staffed by people with the right kind of technical expertise, will guide the masses in the right direction, and will, if necessary, resort to a bit of seduction or mendacity to achieve necessary ends.

In the following passage, Keynes discusses how greedy and befuddled people are, but how they can be gulled through the device of a central bank:

Unemployment develops, that is to say, because people want the moon [i.e., want their wages to be uneconomically high].... There is no remedy but to persuade the public that green cheese [newly printed money] is practically the same thing [as real money] and to have a green cheese factory, (i.e., a central bank) under public control.[169]

What Keynes means is that central banks can bring wages down stealthily by creating inflation. Wages will seem to remain high, but inflation will decrease their purchasing power. In this way, the real value of wages can be reduced without workers understanding what is happening. Keynes was wrong about this; workers do notice what is happening and protest. But the point to be made here is not about whether this works. It is about Keynes's methods, which are guileful and manipulative.

Keynes heirs, generally less witty and less nimble, still run the central banks. The amount of debt that governments, businesses, or consumers take on, they all chorus together, is a purely technical matter. It has nothing to do with morality. Spending and even borrowing in order to spend is good for employment. Leave it to the experts, working stealthily behind closed central bank doors, to ensure that we get neither too much nor too little, but just the right amount. People who criticize all this—who, along with Paul Kasriel, former chief economist for The Northern Trust Company, say that central banks are little more than "legal counterfeiters,"[170] that societies must save in order to become wealthy, that heavily indebted consumers are on a treadmill that will keep them poor forever—these people are just out-of-date.[171]

The Fed's policies are not just a technical matter—far from it. Moral questions are very much involved. For example, is it fair for the Fed to hold interest rates below inflation and thus destroy the purchasing power of average people's savings? Malcolm Bryan, president of the Federal Reserve Bank of Atlanta, asked more than half a century ago (in 1957):

> If a [government] policy of active or permissive inflation is to be a fact...we should have the decency to say to the money saver, "Hold still, Little Fish! All we intend to do is to gut you."[172]

This is only one of the techniques that Keynes referred to jocularly as economic

tricks.

Here is a more complete but still partial list:

- Taking the savings of hard-working people through inflation, as noted by Bryan;
- Pushing savers into speculative securities in order to earn any return;
- Trying to deceive workers by giving them nominal wage gains that leave them less well off;
- Blowing up a housing bubble and in the process luring poor people into default in order to paper over a dot-com bust;
- Feeding Wall Street tycoons with newly printed money at infinitesimal interest rates;
- Bailing out banks and rich people while leaving middle class and poor people to their fate;
- Luring young people into a lifetime of debt to finance an education that probably will not even lead to a job.

For Keynes's immediate Victorian forebears, spending within your means and avoiding debt were moral as well as financial principles. It seems clear that Keynes himself was rebelling against them. He described their

> copybook morality

as

> medieval [and] barbarous

and told his inner circle that

> I remain, and always will remain an
> immoralist.[173]

It was not so long ago that Mr. Micawber's maxim, from Charles Dickens's 19th century novel *David Copperfield*, was generally accepted:

> Annual income twenty pounds, annual
> expenditure nineteen, nineteen six, result
> happiness. Annual income twenty pounds,
> annual expenditure twenty pounds ought
> and six, result misery.

Keynes certainly subverted that idea. In its place, he insinuated the very odd, but now very prevalent idea, that old-fashioned wisdom and morality are out of date, even a bit retarded, and odder still, in conflict with science. This is all nonsense but it now permeates our culture. And the very people who ally themselves with honesty and sustainability outside of economics, for example in environmental stewardship, fail to understand that Keynes is preaching dishonesty and unsustainability in economics.

Gerald P. O'Driscoll, Jr., senior fellow at the Cato Institute, has written that

> free markets depend on truth telling. Prices must reflect the valuations of consumers; interest rates must be reliable guides to entrepreneurs allocating capital across time; and a firm's accounts must reflect the true value of the business. Rather than truth telling, we are becoming an economy of liars.[174]

So we are. The Fed is one of the chief reasons. Shakespeare has King Richard III say:

> Thus I clothe my naked villainy
> With odd old ends, stol'n out of holy writ
> And seem a saint, when most I play the
> devil.

The Fed is no devil. It is doubtless staffed by many sincere people who have no inkling of the moral and financial devastation they are wreaking. But like Richard III, the agency does hide behind a mask, the mask of technocracy, of expertise, of pseudo-science, which gives it much of its undeserved authority.

Any economy is a trust system. It requires a modicum of honesty to survive, and a great deal of honesty to thrive. To thrive again, we must reject the "liar loans" and "liar economy" fueled by the Fed.

27

Is the Fed Even Operating Legally?

OME FED ACTIONS appear to violate the Constitution; others the underlying Fed statute; others fall into a grey area. Taken as a whole, an honest answer to the initial question is that the Fed does appear to be ignoring the law.

1. Article One of the US Constitution states that Congress must authorize government spending. But the Fed budget is not approved by Congress. As previously noted, the Agency simply "prints" new money to pay its expenses in a process that is kept completely secret.

2. We have also noted that the 2010 Dodd-Frank Act created a new executive branch department—

the Consumer Financial Protection Bureau—
and placed it inside the Fed. As a result, the new
department—no different in design than many
other federal regulatory bureaus—will also be
paid for with newly printed money and without
congressional appropriations. Moreover, this new
department, already up to 900 employees and
growing, will shortly cost more than the rest of
the Fed in total.[175]

3. A note to the Fed's Statistical Release H 4.1 (dated
January 6, 2011) revealed that henceforth any losses
incurred from Fed investments in marketable securities would not be charged to the Fed's capital
but would be treated as a liability of the Treasury
Department. This change was not approved by
Congress, and would in any case seem to be uncon-
stitutional, because Congress cannot bestow on
some other body its right and obligation to com-
mit taxpayers' money.

The reason the Fed wanted this change is obvious. Following the Crash of 2008, it began buying
securities of doubtful quality. Moreover, the ratio
of assets to capital of the New York Fed, the system's operating arm, is exceptionally high: 105 at
year end 2011.[176] With so much leverage, three
times the leverage of New York investment banks
going into the Crash, even small losses in securities
purchased could result in a wipe-out of capital,

which would ordinarily mean bankruptcy. It is assumed that, in the event of looming bankruptcy, the Fed would just print more new money for itself. But some lawyer inside the Fed must have warned about the legality of such a move—hence the announcement, equally illegal on the face of it, that henceforth US taxpayers would be responsible for any Fed securities losses.

Of course, it will not be easy to detect any of this. And do not expect to get any information through Freedom of Information Act (FOIA) requests. Fed lawyers have argued that regional banks like the New York Fed are not subject to FOIA because they are really private institutions![177]

4. Article One of the US Constitution also puts Congress in charge of federal borrowing, although the Treasury Department manages it. Many Fed actions since the Crash, including Operation Twist (buying long-term federal debt with proceeds from maturing short-term federal debt) seem to put the Fed illegally in charge of managing the overall US debt structure.

5. When the Fed "prints" new money to buy US government bonds (the government in effect "buys" its own debt), it is not acting illegally. A reading of the underlying Fed statute (originally passed in 1913 and amended since) reveals nothing

that forbids this sleight of hand. It does not make the policy right; it just makes it legal under current law. On the other hand, much of what the Fed did in response to the Crash of 2008 does appear to violate the Fed statute, as pointed out by the economist John P. Hussman.[178]

For example, the Fed violated Section 14(b) of the Federal Reserve Act when it bought $1.5 trillion of Fannie Mae and Freddie Mac mortgage bonds that were not explicitly guaranteed by the US Government. The Agency also falsely relied on Section 13.3 language allowing it to make loans to individuals, partnerships, or corporations

in unusual and exigent circumstances,

because such loans ("discounts") must be short term in nature, for the most part no more than 90 days, and collateralized by high quality securities, conditions that were not met. Many of the Fed loans were held for more than two years and were not backed by the best collateral. As of year-end 2012, the third largest asset category on the Fed's balance sheet was "other," a term for investments which do not seem to fit the requirements of the Fed Statute.[179]

That the Chairman and Board of the Federal Reserve would willfully and explicitly violate the Fed Statute, with hardly any official criticism except from Congressman Ron Paul and a few others, is shocking. In addition, it may be argued that the entire "Too Big to Fail" Wall Street bailout operation mounted by the Fed violated the constitutional rule that only Congress has authority to make fiscal (budget) decisions. It is widely understood that monetary policy is supposed to be aimed at improving conditions of all citizens. When it subsidizes a specific sector or group of individuals, it crosses a line and engages in "fiscal" policy.

Ben Bernanke's own words are instructive about this distinction. In this case, he was speaking about the Bank of Japan:

> In thinking about nonstandard open-market [monetary] operations, it is useful to separate those that have some fiscal component from those that do not. By a fiscal component I mean some implicit subsidy, which would arise, for example, if the BOJ [Bank of Japan] purchased nonperforming bank loans at face value (this is of course equivalent to a fiscal bailout of the banks, financed by the central bank). This [is a] sort of money-financed "gift" to the private sector. . . . Although such operations are perfectly sensible from the standpoint of economic theory, I doubt very much that we will see anything like this in Japan,

> if only because it is more straightforward
> for the Diet to vote subsidies or tax cuts
> directly. Nonstandard open-market oper-
> ations with a fiscal component, even if le-
> gal, would be correctly viewed as an end
> run around the authority of the legislature,
> and so are better left in the realm of theo-
> retical curiosities.[180]

It is noteworthy that what Bernanke labeled a "theoretical curiosity" in 1999 became a principal part of his own actions in 2008.

There are many gaps in our knowledge of what the Fed did during and after the Crash. For example, when the Fed reluctantly agreed to release some data on its actions, half the collateral listed for "Term Securities Lending Facility" loans was missing. Since the collateral was supposed to be AAA-rated securities, one might infer that the Fed chose not to reveal this information for a reason, but it is impossible to be sure without the documentation.[181]

Fed releases also showed that about 70% of dis-count-window loans went to foreign banks at inter-est rates as low as 0.01%.[182] Whether this was legal appears to be a grey area. Fed loans during and after the Crash primarily benefited Wall Street firms, both domestic and foreign owned, including some unexpected ones. Matt Taibbi, who wrote some excellent articles about the Fed for *Rolling Stone*, reported that two Wall Street wives, including the spouse of Morgan Stanley's CEO, formed a real estate investment company which got $220 million of loans, at interest rates that were the equivalent of free money.[183]

6. The Fed is legally charged with setting bank lending reserve requirements. These vary by category of deposit but are currently set at a maximum of 10%, a figure intended to provide banks with a small cushion against losses. The Fed, however, does not appear to be enforcing these rules. Interesting papers on the question of whether the Fed has actually abandoned reserves as a concept have been written by Eric de Carbonnel[184] and Jake Toune.[185]

7. The USA Patriot Act of 2001 established an internal police force for the Fed. Granted, the police force is therefore legal, but do we really want a police force inside an agency that "prints" money for its own needs, is exempted from General Accounting Office or other audits or oversight, and which works in almost complete secrecy? Here is what the Patriot Act provision (Section 364) says:

> Uniform Protection Authority for Federal Reserve: Law enforcement officers designated or authorized by the Board or

a reserve bank under paragraph (1) or (2) are authorized while on duty to carry firearms and make arrests without warrants for any offense against the United States committed in their presence. . . . Such officers shall have access to law enforcement information that may be necessary for the personnel of the Board or a reserve bank.[186]

It will be recalled that in denying Freedom of Information Act requests, Fed lawyers argued that at least the regional Fed banks are "private institutions." So here we have "private institutions" with their own police force, one which may make warrantless arrests.

Part 4

Price Controllers and Crony Capitalists

28

How the Fed Finances Government Growth

THE IMPACT OF Federal Reserve price controls on the economy is even greater than it might at first appear. The obvious influence is on interest rates, including home mortgage rates. More shrouded is the influence on the price of the dollar in relation to other currencies. Virtually opaque is the influence on the quantity of money, which rises as more and more loans are generated with cheap interest rates. Since money is one side of every transaction, all the new money created has a profound effect on prices, with or without any change in official government reported inflation rates.

Even this, however, does not account for the Fed's full impact. Also important is the role of the Fed in financing the expansion of Federal and, to a lesser extent, state and local governments. It is useful to enumerate the different ways in which the agency does so:

- The blowing up of continual bubbles produces large amounts of new tax revenues, at least until the bubbles are succeeded by bust. These bubbles may pervade the economy, as they did during the dot-com or housing bubble, or they may pop up here or there in an otherwise weak economy, as they did after 2008, especially in sectors favored by government stimulus or assistance.

- The suppression of interest rates enables government to borrow larger and larger amounts of money. For the period following the Crash of 2008, the federal government was able to borrow at an interest rate lower than the rate of even official inflation, which was itself suppressed. So, in effect, the government could borrow at no cost at all.

- In addition, the Fed prints money that it uses directly or indirectly to buy federal bonds. This enables the government to borrow from itself.

How ironic that young populists calling themselves "Occupy Wall Street" called the New York [branch of the] Fed

a citadel of capitalism.

Both the Fed and Wall Street are actually citadels of big government.

As we noted earlier in Chapter 10, Thibault de Saint Phalle, author of *The Federal Reserve: An Intentional Mystery*, emphasized the financial dependence of the federal government on the Fed and Wall Street in 1985, long before the Fed money printing machine was fully ginned up by chairmen Alan Greenspan and Ben Bernanke:

> The Fed, by financing the federal deficit year after year, makes it possible for Congress to continue to spend far more than it collects in tax revenue. If it were not for Fed action, Congress would have to curb its spending habits dramatically.[187]

Stanley Druckenmiller, a respected hedge fund manager and economic thinker, made a similar point over a quarter century later:

> One of the many unintended consequences of current monetary policy—and there are many that we don't even know . . . yet— has been a reckless Congress and a reckless

administration with regard to dealing with our fiscal situation down the road. When you cancel price signals from markets— and let's face it, that's what we're doing— we have wage and price control equivalents in the fixed-income markets and, frankly, in all financial markets. We have eliminated the price signals. By eliminating the price signals in the fixed-income market and the stock market, there's no urgency in Congress. . . . The great enabler is quantitative easing, because you're canceling the signal to put enough heat on these [elected] guys to . . . do the right thing.[188]

It is often assumed that big government could finance itself through taxes, if it really needed to do so, that the borrowing from others or itself is just an expedient to get through the next election. But evidence suggests that there are natural limits to the amount of revenue that can be generated by taxation. For example, top federal income tax rates since World War II have varied from a low of 28% (1988–1990) to highs of 94% (1944–1945), 92% (1952–1953), and 91% (1954–1963). By contrast, the percent of total economic output (gross domestic product) consumed by federal taxes has ranged from a low of 15% (2009 after the Crash of 2008) to a high of 21% (in 1944 during wartime), a much narrower band. Even though the top rate fluctuated wildly, the actual revenues produced did not.

The reasons for this are not hard to discern. Even when nominal income tax rates were at 91–92%, earners in the top bracket found ways to pay only an estimated 45% of income, according to the Congressional Research Service, and 31% according to another study.[189] As governments have learned through the ages, the goose does not like to have its feathers plucked, and will find innumerable ways to resist, both passively and actively.

In general, the income tax is only effective because of automatic employee withholding by businesses. Beyond that it is difficult to collect and its growing complexity has not made it easier. National sales taxes might produce more and more reliable revenue, as it does in Europe, where governments take 42% of GDP in France and 37% in Germany, but even this system of taxation could not conceivably pay for all of today's US federal government, especially if all liabilities are included.

Nor is borrowing much of an answer. Following a crash in the 1980s, the Japanese government raised taxes in a variety of ways (for example the capital gains levy was increased on property to 90%), but also borrowed heavily. By 2012 total government debt was more than twice as large as gross domestic product, a level never before reached by a developed nation in world history.

Much of the debt was held by commercial banks, which, as in the United States, were effectively under the control of the government, but in effect both government and banks were insolvent with no apparent way out. The new government elected in 2012 clearly planned to force the central bank to print much more money, which could prevent a default in nominal terms. But paying back loans with an inflated currency is just another form of default.

Is Japan a model for where the United States is headed? It would certainly appear to be. Most of the governments of leading developed nations have grown larger than taxes will support, but governments (unlike businesses) lack a price system to force them to make changes through the threat of immediate bankruptcy.

29

The Crony Capitalist Conundrum

THE FED'S ROLE in enabling government to grow larger than taxes will support has further consequences. A larger government has to justify itself. It does so by promising to right wrongs and help the disadvantaged, which in reality more often than not means helping those who can provide campaign funds or votes. In the process, its tentacles reach deeper and deeper into the economy.

Where once government provided the legal framework for the economy by enacting laws that applied to all equally, and then enforcing those laws, in effect acting as umpire in the economic game, the new and larger government increasingly runs the economy.

And, as it does so, special interests in turn become more and more interested in running government, whether for self-defense or for self-enrichment. Success in this world depends on whom you know in government, not on how well you serve your customers, and huge sums of money flow back and forth between special interests and Washington or other political centers.

Columnist Ross Douthat writes that

> Americans are more likely to fret about Washington's coziness with big business than about big government alone.

But this misses the point. The bigger government becomes, the more all special interests, including unions and lawyers as well as businesses, are drawn to cozy up to it. When government reaches into and tries to run more and more sectors of the economy, the result is not a more equitable or successful economy. It is, instead, an increasingly corrupted economic and political system.

All of this goes under the name crony capitalism, which is an apt description of it. The Federal Reserve, both as price controller and government subsidizer, is a chief enabler of it, but it extends far beyond the Fed, and reaches into almost every nook and cranny of the economy. Consider this list of what private interests currently seek from government, and what a corrupted government in return expects from private interests.

What Private Interests Want from Government:*

- **Exemption from legislation**—e.g., NRA/Sierra Club in Campaign Finance Bill
- **Favorable legislation**—e.g., UPS/Fed Ex battle in Congress, Card Check, Obama proposal to let unemployed sue, rum interests
- **Sales**—e.g., defense, drugs, vaccines, school lunches
- **Regulatory changes**—e.g., health, drugs, housing, banking, finance, agriculture, food, autos, broadcasting, railroads, insurance, trucking, airlines, education, energy, law, accounting
- **Exemption from regulation**—e.g., Obamacare, waivers, family offices under Dodd-Frank, flame retardants
- **Regulation that discourages new or small competitors**—e.g., drugs, supplements, generic drugs, slaughter houses, healthcare
- **Influence over price controls**—e.g., State of Massachusetts medical price controls
- **Access to credit**—e.g., green energy, housing, Wall Street
- **Access to cheap credit**—e.g. banking, housing, finance, consumer finance

---

* For more information on the examples cited, please see this book's companion volume, *Crony Capitalism in America: 2008–2012* (Edinburg, VA: AC2 Books, 2013).

- **Extension of monopoly status**—e.g., patents and copyrights
- **Monopoly status**—e.g., drugs, unions, National Football League, securities rating services
- **Non-competitive bidding on contracts**—e.g., vaccines
- **Direct subsidies**—e.g., education, including union salaries, unions, auto, agriculture, junk food, ethanol, green energy, vaccines, housing (mortgages), AMA, earmarks, high speed rail, fast internet service
- **Indirect subsidies**—e.g., law and accounting both expand with regulations, AARP, Wall Street consultants after Crash, GMO sales to farmers and abroad, mammograms, health insurance mandate, electronic medical records, union dues
- **Bailouts**—e.g., banking, finance, autos, Goldman Sachs
- **Stopping or reversing elimination or phase-out of subsidy**—e.g., fiscal cliff legislation, farm bills
- **Promise of future bailout (which may also reduce current cost of credit)**—e.g., banking, housing, finance
- **Protection from competitors, domestic or foreign**—e.g., trade barriers, currency manipulation

- **Protection from prosecution**—e.g., Goldman Sachs, drug companies, vaccine makers
- **Licensing**—e.g., broadcasting, medical, most professional services, airlines, drugs, law, accounting
- **Tariffs**—e.g., sugar, sugar ethanol
- **Avoidance of being punitively singled out**—e.g., medical device makers in Obamacare
- **Favorable price controls and restrictions**—e.g., Fed control of interest rates, price of farm crop insurance, price of milk, Medicare prices, Medicaid, Obamacare Payment Advisory Board
- **Targeted tax breaks**—e.g., 2009 stimulus bill breaks for Hollywood and World War II Filipino veterans, fiscal cliff legislation, Sandy storm relief
- **Modifications of tax penalties, clawbacks, or phase-outs**—e.g., Pease deductions, Bush tax cuts, loss of subsidies when income rises, in effect a tax on work
- **Prestigious public appointments**

What Public Official Want from Private Interests:

- **Campaign contributions**
- **Direct campaign assistance**
- **Indirect campaign assistance**
- **Assistance with "messaging"**

- **Money** (illegal if takes the form of a bribe, but not necessarily in other cases, e.g., assistance with a loan or access to a "sweetheart" investment)
- **Support from "foundations" related to campaign contributors**
- **Regulatory fees to support agency jobs—** e.g., FDA
- **Jobs for friends, constituents, or eventually self**
- **Travel, entertainment, other "freebies"**
- **Power, control, and deference**

In looking over this laundry list of crony capitalist activity, it is all very damaging, both to the economic and social fabric of a society. The direct price controls, such as the Fed's control of interest rates, are the most damaging from an economic point of view. But all these maneuvers distort prices and thereby undermine a free and truthful price system, which further corrupts all aspects of society.

Keeping government and the rest of society free of corruption is difficult under the best of circumstances. How can we possibly succeed if government intrudes into the day-to-day decisions of business and other private economic interests, such as unions and lawyers, so that the lines drawn between their respective spheres and roles becomes completely blurred?

There is indeed a paradox here. Fearful of private greed, wanting what is best for all, we bring government into ever more minute management of economic as well as political affairs. But in doing so, we do not strengthen our community. Instead we create an epidemic of lying, cheating, theft, and corruption, with more and more people trying to get something for nothing, relying not on what they can do, but on whom they know in government. In surprisingly little time, all the bonds of trust and cooperation nurtured by the free price system become frayed or just disintegrate.

Government's primary job is to protect us from human predators and parasites, and it has a monopoly on the use of force. Who will protect society if the guardians themselves become corrupt and use their power, not to protect us, but for personal gain? Government being a monopoly, we cannot simply turn to a competitor for better service.

30

The Progressive Paradox

I N THE PRIOR chapter, we noted that more government, and especially more government of the economy, produces the unintended consequence of more crony capitalism. This is an especially troublesome point for political progressives, who see more government as a way to control greedy private interests, and also for progressive economists, principally Keynesians, who think that government can rearrange the price system in order to make it work better.

Columnist George Will summarizes the progressive paradox as follows:

> [Progressives] have a rendezvous with regret. Their largest achievement is today's redistributionist government. But such government is inherently regressive: It

tends to distribute power and money to the strong, including itself.

Government becomes big by having big ambitions for supplanting markets as society's primary allocator of wealth and opportunity. Therefore it becomes a magnet for factions muscular enough, in money or numbers or both, to bend government to their advantage.[190]

The 15th–16th century Dutch philosopher and reformer Erasmus wrote that

a city grows[s] rich through the industry of its citizens only to be plundered by the greed of princes.[191]

This was not a complete account. When government plunders, it usually does so in alliance with powerful private interests, which may include prominent citizens or, in a democracy, strategic voter blocs.

How then can government be expected to restrain the special interests with which it is closely allied? The more government "runs" the economy, the more private interests will insinuate themselves into politics and vice versa. Money and power will flow back and forth through ever more corrupted channels. Average citizens will always end up getting the short end of the stick, as they did during and after the Crash of 2008.

Progressive thinkers deal with this paradox in strikingly different ways. Some simply deny the problem. *The Economist* magazine, itself generally progressive, criticized leading progressive (and Keynesian) economist Joseph Stiglitz for taking the easy tack of denial:

> After [Stiglitz] has condemned today's policymakers so roundly as incompetent and beholden to special interests, [his] prescription [for] better regulation . . . and [his] broader faith in government activism sounds perverse. If policymakers failed as miserably as Mr. Stiglitz believes, then he ought to be far more worried about the potential for government failure in the future. That dissonance is a glaring weakness in Mr. Stiglitz's [position].[192]

Economist Bryan Caplan, discussing a book about crony capitalism by the "Marxist" historian Gabriel Kolko, similarly remarked that

> strange as it seems, [Kolko] sees the unholy alliance of business and government as an argument for government.[193]

Progressive economist Jeffrey Sachs at least acknowledges the paradox when he writes, in his book, *The Price of Civilization*, that

> yes, the federal government is incompe-
> tent and corrupt—but we need more, not
> less, of it.

This prompted Congressman Paul Ryan to respond, in a review, that Sach's position

> would be comical if it were not deadly serious.[194]

As previously noted, most progressive economists are dyed-in-the-wool Keynesians. British economist John Maynard Keynes's principal book, *The General Theory of Employment, Interest, and Money*, occupies the same place in progressivism that Karl Marx's *Capital* occupies in communism. One is the "sacred text," obscure enough to require "priestly" interlocutors, the other the actual social system, although it could be argued that Keynes's system may be more accurately described as crony capitalism. This interpretation of Keynesianism as the bible for crony capitalism is supported by Keynes's own explicit admission in *The General Theory* that he was reviving the thinking of mercantilists, early economists from the 16th and 17th centuries who were unabashed apologists for the crony capitalism of their day.

As we have seen throughout this book, Keynes is the best known expositor of today's conventional economic wisdom: the doctrine that economies, especially faltering economies, should be "stimulated" by governments printing new money, driving down interest rates, borrowing the new money back, spending, and when necessary bailing out powerful private interests, although the latter step reflects contemporary Keynesians Alan Greenspan and Ben Bernanke more than Keynes himself. Keynes had assumed that driving down interest rates alone would suffice to pull the US out of the Great Depression.

Keynesianism is replete with vivid paradoxes. A weak economy caused by an alleged glut of savings can be cured by creating more "savings," which is what he called newly printed money. A problem of too much debt can similarly be solved with more debt. Saving and investment were not, as generally thought, the road to wealth. Spending, not saving, makes us rich. Nor do high interest rates encourage savers and saving. Low rates supposedly produce more saving, although, since more saving is undesirable, the prescription of lower and lower rates seems doubly paradoxical.

When confronted by intractable economic problems, Keynes liked to offer big, dramatic ideas, but he also liked what he called

tricks,

ingenious technical solutions that no one else would have contemplated or dared suggest. Confronted with the failure of Keynesian policies either to prevent the Crash of 2008 or to cure its aftermath, and especially confronted with the plague of crony capitalism that has accompanied the expansion of government leadership of the economy on Keynesian lines, some of Keynes's disciples have responded with some proposed "tricks" of their own. In each instance, the gist of the advice is that government should double down by taking an even larger role in running the economy and influencing or controlling prices. Two of these proposals we have previously mentioned:

- Accelerate creation of new money to drive up consumer price index inflation, perhaps to as high as 6%. Meanwhile continue to control interest rates, holding short rates to near zero, by using the new money to buy securities. The idea is to encourage new borrowing and spending by virtually giving money away at—6% real (inflation adjusted) rates. (Gregory Mankiw, Harvard).[195]
- Develop a desired level of borrowing (and spending) for the economy each year, and then take whatever actions would guarantee that this level is reached. (George Akerlof, UC, Berkeley, and Robert Shiller, Yale).[196]

Other proposals include the following:

- Raise taxes on employers and those holding jobs and use the proceeds to encourage hiring, in particular by subsidizing $4.50 of each new low income worker's wage. (Robert Shiller, Yale).[197]

- Issue new government securities that will never be repaid. (Robert Shiller, Yale).[198]

- Call on workers and employers to reduce wages by 7.5%, use the proceeds to hire new workers, and repay the existing workers with company stock or future profit sharing equal to the 7.5% of wages they gave up. (Lawrence Kotlikoff, Boston University, 2011).[199]

- Put economists in charge of deciding which industries have prices and wages that are too high, then intervene to reduce them. (Kotlikoff, 2011).

- Compel or persuade everyone to take an uncompensated 10% pay cut, with employers putting all this money into new hiring. (Ken Mayland, president, Clear View Economics).[200]

- Set taxes so that the income of the top 1% of households will never be more than 36x the median household income. Everything above that level will be taxed away. (Ian Ayres, Yale, and Aaron S. Edlin, UC, Berkeley).[201]

- [If additional monetary stimulus is needed], abolish paper money, replace it with electronic accounts that will be subject to a reverse rate of interest to encourage spending, and use newly printed money to buy assets other than government securities, in order to overcome

> institutional conservatism, [and] a lack of coordination and cooperation between monetary and fiscal authorities due to a range of political dysfunctionalities. (Willem Buiter and Ebrahim Rahbari, Citigroup economists).[202]

■ The Bank of Japan, which has previously used newly printed money to "buy" government bonds, should print even more money and use it to "buy"

> physical assets such as real estate, . . . airports, sports stadiums, rice farms, dormant nuclear reactors, golf courses, universities, entire villages . . . , you name it . . . get creative. (William Pesek, economic writer based in Tokyo).[203]

Rather than follow Keynes and his followers down all these rabbit holes, let us ask ourselves: are there some common themes to these schemes? And there are. The first common theme is that market prices do not matter. No free price or profit relationship should be left alone. The price/profit system should be pulled completely apart and left to economists to try to reassemble it in some fashion.

And what about crony capitalism? How will all these schemes help rein in the corruption that just deepens as the government dismantles the free price system? We do not hear this question even being asked, much less answered. Robert Skidelsky, ardent Keynesian and author of a definitive three volume Keynes biography, says that

> The system of the past 30 years . . . has . . . benefit[ed] a predatory plutocracy that creams off the riches.[204]

Well, yes. But what he completely fails to notice is how complicit Keynesianism is in the creation of this corrupt crony capitalist system.

At least the leading Keynesians cited above recognize the need for change. Many progressives, confronted by the problems presented by their own system, have (paradoxically again) become reactionaries opposed to any change. Here is what Southern Methodist University (SMU) health policy analyst and anti-Keynesian John Goodman said about progressive voters after the 2012 presidential election:

> If you are one of the folks who voted [as a progressive] in the last election, what did you vote for? . . . Here are three things for starters: (1) no reform of the public schools, (2) no reform of the welfare systems, and (3) no reform of labor market institutions

that erect barriers between new entrants and good jobs. . . .

The first three policies you voted for mean that those on the bottom rung of the income ladder are not going to get a helping hand to get on a higher rung. As far as those with the least income and wealth are concerned, you voted for status quo all the way. And to rub salt in the wound, the very people you voted for will be telling the world at every opportunity how much they care about the poor—even as they do everything to impede their economic mobility!

Here are three more things you voted for: (1) no reform of the tax system, (2) no reform of Social Security, Medicare, Medicaid and other entitlements, and (3) no serious effort to deal with mounting deficit spending and ever-increasing national debt. . . .

The second set of policies you voted for adds up to another bottom line: with respect to the nation's fiscal health, you voted again for status quo all the way. There is no mystery about the problem we face. We've promised more than we can afford. According to the Congressional Budget Office, if we continue on the path we are on the federal government will need to collect two-thirds of the income of the middle class and more than 90% of the income of high-income families by mid-century.

The idea of progressives as reactionaries will be an affront to most progressives, but where the shoe fits, they will have to wear it. Nor is it the most searing indictment. An even more disturbing idea is that many progressives, like many late 20th century Soviet Communists, have lost their faith and, behind a mask of superficial pieties, are mainly focusing on what side their bread is buttered. On anything from a small to a large scale, they have become crony capitalists themselves.

People in this category include:

- Progressive teachers who mainly focus on getting higher pay or who talk up a lottery for education, even though lotteries just take money from those who have least;
- Progressive union members fighting against jobs going overseas where other workers may be much more desperately needy;
- Or progressive seniors who do not mind being subsidized by young people who are on average the poorest group of all.

In these instances, the alleged reformers may be talking the old talk, but they seem to have found a comfortable spot in the crony capitalist system. They have traveled a long distance from what may have been the idealism of their youth, still mirrored in the young people who intensely protest against what they call "capitalism," communicating through their iPhones, digging up information on the internet with iPads, or meeting up at Starbucks to recharge with costly varieties of caffeine, all with little or no perceived irony, but at least with a still untainted sincerity.

The essence of the problem with all these versions of progressivism was partly captured by investor and author Jim Rogers when he wrote that

> governments are terrible at engendering prosperity and wealth.[205]

But it must be added that these efforts to create prosperity and wealth more often than not create corruption, and nothing is more deadly for sustained prosperity than corruption.

However well-intentioned progressive ideas of government leading the economy may be, they always entail dismantling of the price system, and this will not work. By now this should be clear enough. Endlessly repeating the errors of the recent past will just make things worse, much worse. Treasury Secretary Henry Morgenthau, President Franklin Roosevelt's close friend and heartfelt progressive, admitted in 1939 that government leadership of the economy had not rescued us from the Great Depression:

> I want to see this country prosperous. I want
> to see people get enough to eat. We have
> never made good on our promises ... I say
> after eight years of this administration we
> have just as much unemployment as when
> we started and an enormous debt to boot.[206]

Walter Lippmann, another famous progressive who believed deeply in the promise of government economic leadership, finally agreed in 1943 that it tended to produce the opposite of what was intended:

> This is the vicious paradox of the gradual
> collectivism which has developed in west-
> ern society during the past sixty years: it
> has provoked the expectation of univer-
> sal plenty provided by action of the state
> while, through almost every action under-
> taken or tolerated by the state, the produc-
> tion of wealth is restricted.[207]

The customary progressive response to Lippmann's plaintive observation is that we just need an even stronger dose of the same medicine. But this defies logic. Lippmann was reporting on sixty years of free price destruction; we have had almost seventy more years since. It is time to face reality and move on.

Intellectual revolutions are always hard fought and the fighting takes a long time to play out. Social and economic establishments are determined to preserve their privileges. At first they mock their critics; any argument for reform, however factual or logical, is greeted with derision. What a joke! Once it becomes clear that the other side is making its case and starting to gain a foothold with the voting public, mockery is succeeded by stony silence. Everything the critics say is now ignored, lest more people hear about it. In the next stage, the established elite finally acknowledges its critics and comes out battling, using every device at hand to try to destroy them. If this fails, and the critics finally win the battle of public opinion, the old elite simply says: "Oh, we knew that all along."

Today the progressive elites are feeling besieged. They are no longer just mocking their critics. They are finding it more and more difficult to ignore them. The third stage battle seems to have been joined, with the final result still to be seen.

31

Where Does This Leave the Poor?

IN EARLIER CHAPTERS, we have discussed how the Federal Reserve finances the expansion of government and also helps make Wall Street rich. Managers of big corporations also benefit from Fed maneuvers. The massive deficits of the federal government that are financed by the Fed boost corporate profits. This is why, in the aftermath of the Crash of 2008, historically very high corporate profits existed right alongside glacial economic growth and high unemployment. Indeed, the high unemployment helped to keep wages low, so that profits were further boosted by low wage costs.

It got even better for corporate insiders. They could also borrow the Fed's newly printed money at negligible rates, and use the proceeds of the loans to buy in company stock. This was supposed to help shareholders by increasing earnings per share, but really helped the managers and other insiders offset and render invisible the stock dilution caused by their own cheap share options awards. Share repurchases also helped keep the share price high, so that the options would be valuable when exercised.

In sharp contrast, US workers' wages have been stagnant or falling in real (inflation adjusted terms) for many years. But it is the future of worker's wages that is especially bleak. Ask yourself a simple question. Why are US workers paid more than those in most other countries? The answer is that they are more productive.

And why are they more productive? Partly because they are better educated, although that advantage is eroding. A more important difference is that American workers have more investment capital behind them— capital that has been put in place precisely to increase productivity or improve quality. Note, however, that as the Fed prints new money, and companies borrow to buy in their stock, the one thing they are not doing is investing in the new plant and equipment needed to pay for the future wage gains of workers.

American consumers and companies have saved and invested in recent decades, although at a reduced rate compared to history. And much of that has been lost in fruitless bubbles that came and went. Too much of what remains consists of bubble assets or firms that should have been liquidated, but have instead been propped up by bailouts or crony-ridden regulations.

By now, what the government calls private gross domestic investment is actually lower than in the late 1990s. At this rate, American workers are living on borrowed time, because they are using older, no longer cutting edge capital. How long will it take developing countries to overtake our wages, either because US wages fall or other countries' wages rise? That completely depends on whether the US stops relying on the Fed's toxic money printing presses and instead starts to save and invest—not only save and invest, but invest wisely in legitimate, well-chosen enterprises.

No one really benefits from our present Fed-financed crony capitalist world. Even the seeming beneficiaries—government, Wall Street, big corporations—are just sowing the seeds of their own future destruction. In the meantime, however, it is the middle class, and the poor most of all, who pay the price.

Yes, there is the "social safety net," the array of government programs for the poor which has greatly expanded since the Crash of 2008. Of that "net," GOP candidate Mitt Romney said during the 2012, presidential campaign:

> I'm not concerned about the very poor.
> We have a safety net there. If it needs re-
> pair, I'll fix it.[208]

Does this "net" need fixing? A Senate subcommit-
tee found that the US government in 2012 was making "welfare" payments equivalent to $168 per day for
every household whose income fell below the official
poverty line. Since median income of all Americans is
$137 a day, it is clear that only a small part of the $168
(equivalent to about $36,000 a year) is actually reach-
ing the poor.

Much of the money is going to other people,
including government workers who, supported by
powerful public unions, are indirect but prime beneficiaries of poverty programs. Looking at all government transfer payments, not just those included in
the congressional study, only 36% of the money goes
to the bottom 20% of earners and even less to the
truly poor.[209] The greater part of the money goes to
households headed by 65 year olds or older whose net
worth is a stunning 47 times greater than households
headed by under 35 year olds.[210]

Another feature of the welfare spending is that it
does not just create disincentives to work. It actually taxes work at a far higher rate than that applied
through the regular tax code. As economist Thomas
Sowell has pointed out, a low income individual may
find that the next $10,000 of earned income will

reduce federal benefits by $15,000, which in effect represent a 150% "tax" rate.[211] This is completely unfair, but remains largely unacknowledged, much less addressed, by public policy.

When thinking about welfare spending, we should also ask: where does the money come from? In part, it comes from taxes paid by higher income earners. But much of it is borrowed. When the time comes to pay the interest or repay the debt, who will receive the money—rich or poor? It will be the rich of course, either rich Americans or rich foreigners or foreign central banks. It will not be the poor.

Other government policies do not make things better. The federal minimum wage was raised in steps to $7.25 during and after the Crash of 2008. This hurt impoverished, inexperienced young workers the most, so why would anyone be surprised that the teenage unemployment rate rose to 26% in 2009, 39% for black teenagers, and 52% for all teenagers in Washington, DC?

Obamacare compounded this problem by adding $2.28-$5.89 of cost per hour for every full-time worker and more for part-time. How can an uneducated worker gain the experience and track record needed to earn such wages without work? And yet how can he or she get the work with such mandated wages? If they are lucky, teenagers work today as "interns" for nothing. Why not at least allow a "training wage," so that idle teenagers could both learn and earn?

Obamacare also encourages the creation of Accountable Care Organizations, where medical professionals are paid for health "outcomes" rather than on a fee for service basis. Because low income patients tend to have worse "outcomes," ACOs will likely respond by trying to minimize the number of such patients. Poor patients in many areas already find it nearly impossible to find a doctor who will take Medicaid payments, and the majority of newly insured individuals and families under Obamacare will be offered Medicaid as their sole alternative. Some poor people will doubtless fail to sign up for Medicaid. Is any provision made for them? No, none whatever.

There is an even more basic problem for the poor. Each year, the price of everything increases. In part, the price increases are directly caused by government rules and mandates. Recently, the federal government required the installation of a "black box" in each automobile, which will give speed (and other potentially incriminating information) in the event of a crash. Like other government requirements, this will increase the price of a car, making it that much harder for the poor to buy one.

The "cash for clunkers" program created after the Crash of 2008 was supposed to assist both the automobile companies and low income buyers, and to reduce car pollution as well. It mostly produced a lot of unintended consequences. First, it greatly reduced used car supply, so that those prices rose, shutting out poor buyers. Second, it resulted in many poor quality loans that were followed by repossession. The buyer had lost his or her used car and now had no car at all. And, finally, it led to more air pollution, not less, because of the way that car disposal rules were written. Parts that could have been recycled were not, for fear of cheating, but were instead incinerated.

Government licensing requirements raise the cost of even the most basic services for the poor. Hair-cutting costs more, because employees are not allowed to learn by doing, but must take expensive, prescribed courses. Childcare costs much more because the neighbor down the street is no longer allowed to take your children for the day in return for a payment. These rules are all introduced as consumer protections, but more often than not protect cartels of service providers, and invariably raise prices, which hurts the poor most directly. Even the ability of the poor to escape the ghetto is impeded by rules against "gypsy" car services. And when local and state governments keep expanding to create and enforce these rules, the sales taxes may go up, which also hit the poor hardest.

As important as all these price elevators are, they are not the chief way that government raises prices for the poor. As we have pointed out in earlier chapters, the free price system tends to drive down prices, while incontinent federal money creation keeps driving them up.

This is not especially hard on the rich. They generally know how to protect themselves or even turn the inflation to their advantage by making shrewd investments in sectors where the new money created by the Fed is blowing up bubbles. Meanwhile the middle class and the poor must work harder and harder to afford the same standard of living or, more likely, face a declining standard of living.

There are no lack of excuses for what inflation does to the poor. Alan Blinder, vice-chairman of the Fed under President Bill Clinton, says that

> the harm [which] inflation inflicts on the economy is often exaggerated.[212]

Blinder seems to think that lowering interest rates by printing more money will increase economic growth, that this will help the poor and reduce income inequality, and that inflation is a small price to pay for these gains. But none of this is actually true. Thwarting free prices, relentlessly and mindlessly interfering with interest rates and currencies in particular, leads to chronic instability and job destruction. Rising prices just add further to the miseries of the poor, as numerous studies have shown.[213] Domingo Cavallo, Finance Minister of Argentina in the 1990s, was right when he stated that the poor are the foremost victims of inflation, followed only by the middle class.

A variant of Blinder's argument has been voiced by Christina Romer, president Obama's first Chairman of the Council of Economic Advisors. Money printing, she says

> tends to lower the price of the dollar [which is] good for ordinary families.[214]

The basic idea here is that consumer goods from China will be cheaper. What this ignores is that other countries will print just as much or more money in response, de facto currency devaluations will escalate endlessly, and, again, bubble and bust will follow, producing mainly unemployment and suffering for the poor.

If we are at all serious about ending poverty, much less improving the plight of the poor, we need to acknowledge the utter perversity of what we are doing today, and find a new way forward. Instead of focusing mostly on the gap between rich and poor, that is, relative poverty, we should focus more on absolute poverty, on getting people to a safe and reasonably comfortable standard of living that opens up choices and opportunities. There is not that much difference between having enough money and having an infinite amount of it. The goal should be to get everyone to "enough." Government policy should support this by leaving prices free to do their job, not thwart it with toxic price manipulations and controls.

Part 5

Reform

32

Real Reform 1:
Abolish the Fed

THE FEDERAL GOVERNMENT regulates the economy, not just with laws, as the Constitution intended, but with opaque and endlessly proliferating rules. Wall Street employees are required to sign statements saying that they understand the rules, but in truth no one really understands the rules, not even the multitude of lawyers hired at high prices for their guidance.

Ironically, the Federal Reserve, the Government's chief financier, as well as Wall Street regulator, does not believe in regulation of itself. Rules imposed by others, or even audits, are dismissed as too restrictive. Economic analyst Ned Davis notes:

> They . . . argue [that] they are smarter than
> the rules and need flexibility.[215]

The Fed prints as much money as it likes, anytime it
likes. In the words of economist Ed Yardeni, it

> operate[s] an open bar for the fiscal drunks
> in Washington.[216]

Dylan Grice, an economist at Société Générale,
underscores the unfairness, as well as the economic
wrong-headedness of what is happening:

> The Fed doesn't expand the money sup-
> ply by uniformly dropping cash from he-
> licopters over the hapless masses. Rather,
> it directs capital . . . to the largest banks.
> [This] result[s] in immediate handouts
> to the financial elite first, in the hope
> that they will subsequently unleash this
> fresh capital on to the unsuspecting mar-
> kets, raising demand and prices wherever
> they do. The Fed, having gone on an un-
> precedented credit expansion spree, has
> benefited the recipients who were first
> in line at the trough: banks . . . and those
> favored entities and individuals deemed
> most creditworthy.[217]

Steve Forbes, editor-in-chief of *Forbes* magazine,
adds that

what the Fed is doing through its binge [money printing] is enabling Washington to consume our national wealth. Instead of creating new wealth, we are beginning to destroy that which exists. No wonder tens of millions of people feel—rightly— that their real incomes are declining. . . .[218]

John Tamny, also writing in *Forbes*, is blunter:

The Fed's actions are those of a child placed in the driver's seat of the family car.[219]

Unfortunately, there is little reason to suppose that the Fed will voluntarily choose to turn back from its present course. Because Senate Democrats refused to confirm George W. Bush's later appointments, all seven members of the board were appointed (or in the case of Bernanke reappointed) by President Obama, an enthusiastic supporter of what the Fed has been doing. These appointments are for fourteen years, although some recent appointees are filling unexpired terms, and thus will not serve that long. In any case, history suggests that powerful central banks do not often change course unless forced to do so by the inflation or economic bust that their policies have created.

An interesting exception to this rule was the abolition of the Second Bank of the United States, which served as the US's central bank (1817–1836). The

First Bank of the United States had been chartered
by Congress in 1701 during the Washington administration over the opposition of Thomas Jefferson and
James Madison. Jefferson warned:

> I sincerely believe . . . that banking estab-
> lishments are more dangerous than stand-
> ing armies,[220]

And a renewal of the bank's charter failed by one vote
in the House and Senate in 1811 during Madison's first
term as president.

By the end of his second term, Madison was strug-
gling to finance the government following the War
of 1812, and agreed to create the Second Bank of the
United States for another twenty-year term. President
Andrew Jackson in 1832 vetoed a renewal of the charter, and in doing so sent to Congress a remarkable message, one as relevant for the 21st century as the 19th:

> It is to be regretted that the rich and pow-
> erful too often bend the acts of government
> to their selfish purposes. Distinctions in
> society will always exist under every just
> government. Equality of talents, of edu-
> cation, or of wealth cannot be produced
> by human institutions. In the full enjoy-
> ment of the gifts of Heaven and the fruits
> of superior industry, economy, and virtue,

every man is equally entitled to protection by law; but when the laws undertake to add to these natural and just advantages artificial distinctions, to grant titles, gratuities, and exclusive privileges, to make the rich richer and the potent more powerful, the humble members of society—the farmers, mechanics, and laborers—who have neither the time nor the means of securing like favors to themselves, have a right to complain of the injustice of their Government.

Many of our rich men have not been content with equal protection and equal benefits, but have besought us to make them richer by act of Congress. . . . It is time to pause in our career to review our principles. . . . If we cannot at once, in justice to interests vested under improvident legislation, make our Government what it ought to be, we can at least take a stand against all new grants of monopolies and exclusive privileges, against any prostitution of our Government to the advancement of the few at the expense of the many. . . .[221]

Jackson does not mention in his formal message that he was also suspicious of the role of central banks in blowing up economic bubbles. He had apparently intuited this central truth of monetary economics by reading about the South Sea Bubble in France (1711–1720). Unfortunately, he failed to see that central banks and related attempts of government to manipulate the currency are not the sole cause of bubbles, that fractional reserve banking practices were also at fault. But he was right that eliminating central banks would make bubbles more self-limiting and thus less potentially catastrophic.

The way forward for the US or any nation is to abolish both central banks and fractional reserve banking. That would of course be immensely difficult. There is intellectual error to be overcome. There are also vested interests to be fought, the same sort of vested interests which tried every means, including bribery, to destroy Jackson, and which have grown ever fatter and more powerful under today's Fed.

Jackson reminds us that

> if we cannot at once . . . make our government what it ought to be, . . . we should still do everything we can do to restore just principles.

A start would be to break the Fed's monopoly on domestic money by allowing competing currencies, as suggested in Chapter 22.

Ron Paul, congressman, GOP presidential candidate, and author of *End the Fed*, specified the required legislative steps in his Free Competition in Currency Act of 2011, including an end to federal, state, or local taxes on gold and silver bullion, so that these metals could be freely used in monetary transactions. Confronted with competition from sound money, which cannot be endlessly reproduced at the flick of a computer key, the Fed as we know it would either have to change or die. Better to abolish it at one stroke, as Jackson abolished the central bank of his day, but if that is not possible, Paul's Act would in the long run accomplish much the same thing.

33

Real Reform 2:
Free Prices[*]

AS IMPORTANT AS it is to abolish the Fed, it is only the start of a complete program of economic reform. That reform should be guided by one overarching principle: that prices must be free, fully emancipated from government. If prices are set by consumer choice, not by continual government intervention, the economy can begin to heal itself, grow, and eventually free everyone, not just the fortunate few, from the shackles of poverty.

Each and every government action relating to the economy should be evaluated on this one criterion at least: does it confuse, manipulate, or control prices? If

[*] Portions of this chapter also appear at the conclusion of *Crony Capitalism in America: 2008-2012*, this book's companion volume.

so, it should be rejected. Free prices should always be the banner beneath which today's reformers march.

Free prices should not be confused with an abandonment of principles of social justice. Our original constitutional system embraced the ideal of government as social and economic umpire, enforcing the rules against force and fraud and disavowal of contracts. Banning child labor or inhuman working conditions is legitimately part of the umpire's role and does not interfere with prices.

The early laissez-faire reformers generally agreed. British M. P. Richard Cobden (1804–1865), one of the principal leaders of the movement, wanted to get government out of a leadership role in the economy, but voted for restrictions on child labor as well as for more child education. Like other laissez-faire reformers, he also fought for broadening the right to vote, the removal of restrictions on Jews, and against slavery.[222]

Our constitutional system was never perfect. The first law passed by Congress was an import Tariff Act which both interfered with prices and rewarded special interests, the crony capitalists of the day. But over time, the early mistakes were compounded by the wholly fallacious belief that government could improve on the free price system by manipulating and controlling it, indeed by subverting it. What a paradoxical doctrine, that the economy can be improved by destroying the price mechanism on which it depends.

Ben Bernanke, chairman of the Fed, would super-ficially seem to agree. He tells students in a university economics class that

> prices are the thermostat of an economy. They are the mechanisms by which an economy functions.[223]

But then he radically expands the price fixing reach of the Fed from short-term interest rates to all kinds of interest rates.

At the same time, the federal government, sup-ported and financed by the Fed, expands its own myriad price manipulations, monopolies, and sub-sidies. It incorporates a "fall-back" price control feature in the Affordable Care Act (Obamacare). State governments follow suit. For example, Massachusetts amends its "Romneycare universal health plan" by passing a medical price control law in 2012,[224] a law that requires government approval not only of price changes, but of all "material" changes by healthcare providers. In each case, price controls are expanded as a remedy for ills created in the first place by earlier price manipulations and controls.

These are obvious examples, but on close examina-tion almost everything the government does in trying to lead the economy involves a price manipulation or control. It is time to pay heed to some sensible advice from humorist P. J. O'Rourke:

[The free price system] is a bathroom scale. We may not like what we see when we step on the bathroom scale, but we can't pass a law making ourselves weigh 165.[225]

In Chapter 14, we noted that

a thriving economy is comprised of billions of prices and trillions of price relationships. Left alone, these prices almost miraculously coordinate demand with supply so that buyers can obtain as much as possible of what they want. Refusing to let prices fall or pushing them higher (2% a year, now 2.5% a year, according to the Fed's announced target, linked to an artificial and dubious index) is like jamming a stick into the spokes of a wheel or pouring sand in the fuel tank of an engine. If we do this, we should not wonder if the wheel ceases to turn or the engine refuses to run.

Price manipulations and controls do not just destroy efficiency, wealth creation, and the hope of improvement for those in poverty. They also foster crony capitalist corruption, and thus undermine the truthtelling and moral behavior on which all economic relations depend.

In the introduction, we quoted Norwegian business executive Oystein Dahle's insight that

> [Soviet] socialism collapsed because it did not allow prices to tell the economic truth.[226]

We further observed that

> the most reliable barometer of economic honesty is to be found in prices. Honest prices, neither manipulated nor controlled, provide both investors and consumers with reliable economic signals. . . .

> A corrupt economic system does not want honest prices, honest information, or honest results. The truth may be inconvenient or unprofitable for powerful government leaders or private interests allied with them.

Both our economic and our political system have become increasingly corrupt. We need to allow prices to tell the truth, free from the self-dealing and self-interested theories that stand in their way.

In 1939, a South African economist named William Hutt made an interesting observation:

> The clue to the understanding of the chief economic and sociological problems of today can be found in my opinion, in a recognition of the struggle which is in progress against the disrupting equalitarian effects of [the free price system]. Competition and [the free price system] are hated

today because of their tendency to destroy poverty and privilege more rapidly than custom and the expectations established by protections can allow. We accordingly find private interests combining to curb this process and calling upon the State to step in to do the same; and unless the resistance is expressed through monetary policy, the curbing takes the form of restrictions on production.[227]

Hutt's view is radical, but he has a point. Free prices are continually under attack by vested interests. We need to defend them and by doing so become ever more cooperative and productive. This potentially helps the poor most of all.

Is it possible that one reform proposal—free prices applied logically, systematically, and courageously—can free us from the economic stagnation and corruption of the past, thereby opening up an economic future for everyone, not just the rich and powerful? Yes it is. Even the arch enemy of free prices, economist John Maynard Keynes, agreed that

ideas rule the world.[228]

It was not so long ago that humanity condemned economic competition and described economic change as evil. No wonder economic progress was unknown. Born poor, we died poor, with the limited exception of those few who controlled weapons and could take what they wanted. It was the gradual discovery of the power of free prices, beginning especially before the so-called industrial revolution, that allowed for the advancement of living standards even with population growth.

As Walter Lippmann noted in his book 1943 book, *The Good Society*:

> Until the division of labor had begun to make men dependent upon the free collaboration of other men, the worldly policy was to be predatory. The claims of the spirit were other-worldly. So it was not until the industrial revolution [made possible by the free price system] had altered the traditional mode of life that the vista was opened at the end of which men could see the possibility of the Good Society on this earth. At long last the ancient schism between the world and the spirit, between self-interest and disinterestedness, was potentially closed, and a wholly new orientation of the human race became theoretically conceivable and, in fact, necessary.[229]

A contemporary Chinese economist, Zhang Weiying, famous for his opposition to Keynesian economic policies and crony capitalism, reminds us that

we human beings always seek happiness.
Now there are two ways. You make yourself
happy by making other people unhappy—
I call that the logic of robbery. The other
way, you make yourself happy by making
other people happy—that's the logic of [co-
operation through free prices in] the market. Which way do you prefer?[230]

Which way do we prefer? For our own sake, for
the sake of the poor, and for the sake of our descen-
dants, it is time to rediscover the power of free prices
and re-commit to reform.

Free prices now!

Endnotes

1. Lester Brown press release, November 6, 2001.

2. Anne Robert Jacques Turgot, *Eloge de Gournay* (1770); also in Denis Thomas, *The Mind of Economic Man* (Kent, UK: Quadrangle Books, 1970), 158.

3. John Maynard Keynes, BBC Broadcast (March 14, 1932), in *Collected Writings*, vol. 21, *Activities 1931–39: World Crisis and Policies in Britain and America* (London: Macmillan; New York: St. Martin's Press, 1982), 86, 92.

4. Ludwig von Mises, *Human Action: A Treatise on Economics* (Chicago: Henry Regnery Company, 1966), 721.

5. Henry Hazlitt, *The Wisdom of Henry Hazlitt* (Irving-on-Hudson: Foundation for Economic Education, 1993), 86.

6. Ted Honderich, *After the Terror* (Edinburgh: Edinburgh University Press, 2002), 137-38; cited in *Mises Review 9*, no.1 (Spring 2003): 15–16.

7. Karl Marx and Friedrich Engels, *The Communist Party Manifesto* (1848).

8. Howard Zinn, Emeritus Professor of History, Boston University and author of American history texts and other books, internet interview by David Barsamion, Boulder, CO, November 11, 1992.

9. Ludwig von Mises, *Economic Policy: Thoughts for Today and Tomorrow* (Lake Bluff, IL: Regnery Gateway, 1985), 3.

10. Milton Friedman, *Capitalism and Freedom* (Chicago: University of Chicago Press, 1962), 170.

11. Milton and Rose Friedman, *Free to Choose: A Personal Statement* (New York: Avon, 1981), 138.

12. Henry Hazlitt, *The Conquest of Poverty* (Irvington-on-Hudson, NY: Foundation for Economic Education, 1994), 51.

13. Mises, *Economic Policy*, 1.

14. Edwin Cannan, *An Economist's Protest* (New York: Adelphi Company, 1928), 429.

15. Mises, *Economic Policy*, 20.

16. Ibid.

17. A term coined by Michael Polanyi (1951); also see Sanford Ikeda, *Dynamics of the Mixed Economy: Toward a Theory of Interventionism* (London and New York: Routledge, 1997), 256 passim.

18. Walter Lippmann, *Interpretations: 1931–1932* (New York: Macmillan Company, 1932), 38.

19. Friedrich A. Hayek, "The Use of Knowledge in Society," *American Economic Review*, 35:4 (September 1945): 519–30. Reprinted in Friedrich A. Hayek, *Individualism and Economic Order* (Chicago: Henry Regnery Company, 1972), 77–91.

20. Adam Smith, *The Wealth of Nations*, bk. IV, chap. 2 (Edinburgh, 1776); also in G. Bannock, R. E. Baxter, and R. Reef, *The Penguin Dictionary of Economics* (London: Penguin Books, 1972), 247.

21. Robert Skidelsky, *John Maynard Keynes*, vol. 2, *The Economist as Savior 1920–1937* (London: Macmillan, 2000), 233.

22. John Maynard Keynes, *The General Theory of Employment, Interest, and Money* (Amherst, NY: Prometheus Books, 1997), 372.

23. Norman Cott, *Free Market* (January 2003): 7.

24. *Forbes* (March 16, 1992): 64.

25. Arthur Okun, *Fortune* (November 1975): 199.

26. Friedman, *Free to Choose*, 137.

27. *Forbes* (August 6, 2001): 77.

28. Wilhelm Röpke, *Economics of the Free Society* (Chicago: Henry Regnery Company, 1963), 235.

29. Cited by economic expert Lawrence Siegel in a paper (November 27, 2012). Siegel says this may or may not be true but cites Kofi Annan, former secretary general of the UN, Al Gore, and Newt Gingrich.

30. Marx and Engels, *Communist Manifesto*.

31. P. T. Bauer, *Equality, the Third World, and Economic Delusion* (Cambridge, MA: Harvard University Press, 1981), 9.

32. Ibid., 10.

33. John Maynard Keynes, *Essays in Persuasion* (New York: W. W. Norton, 1963), 372.

34. Smith, *Wealth of Nations*, bk. 1, chap. 2, 20.

35. Ibid., bk. 4, 352.

36. *John Hussman Letter*, (December 3, 2012).

37. Adam Smith, *Lectures on Justice, Police, Revenue, and Arms*, 253–5; also in Cannan, *An Economist's Protest*, 425.

38. Adam Smith, *The Theory of Moral Sentiments*, 464–6; also in Cannan, *An Economist's Protest*, 425.

39. George Stigler, *The Intellectual and the Market Place*, (Glencoe, IL: Free Press, 1963); also in Thomas, *Mind of Economic Man*, 148.

40. Geoffrey Martin Hodgson, *Economics and Utopia* (New York: Routledge, 1999), pt. III, 256; also in Charles Robert McCann, ed., *The Elgar Dictionary of Economic Quotations*, (Northampton, MA: Edward Elgar, 2003), 75.

41. Letter to editor of Smith College campus newspaper, *Forbes* (July 21, 2003), 52.

42. *Deflation . . . What If*, Leuthold Group (December 2002).

43. M. Deane and R. Pringle, *The Central Banks* (London: Hamish Hamilton, 1994), n.p.; also in James Grant, *The Trouble with Prosperity: The Loss of Fear, the Rise of Speculation, and the Risk to American Savings* (New York: Times Books, 1996), 198.

44. See John Williams, http://www.shadowstats.com.

45. *Kurt Richebacher Letter* (August 2006), also quoted in Marc Faber, *Gloom, Boom, and Doom Report* (August 2012), 9.

46. For a more complete discussion, see Hunter Lewis, *Are the Rich Necessary? Great Economic Arguments and How They Reflect Our Personal Values* (Mt. Jackson, VA: Axios Press, 2009), Appendix C, 241.

47. Friedman, *Free to Choose*, 258.

48. Murray Rothbard, *The Case Against the Fed* (Auburn, AL: Ludwig von Mises Institute, 1994), 11, 145.

49. *Business Week* (May 20, 1985): 38.

50. J. S. Mill, *Essays on Some Unsettled Questions of Political Economy* (1830, 1844); also in Henry Hazlitt, *Failure of the "New Economics": An Analysis of the Keynesian Fallacies* (New Rochelle, NY: Arlington House, 1978), 367.

51. Henry Hazlitt, *Failure of the "New Economics"*, 372.

52. Henry Hazlitt, *The Inflation Crisis, and How to Resolve It* (New Rochelle, NY: Arlington House, 1978), 79.

53. Jeff Madrick, *New York Review of Books* (May 3, 2001): 42.

54. Gottfried Haberler, in Ludwig von Mises, and others, *The Austrian Theory of the Trade Cycle* (Auburn, AL: Ludwig von Mises Institute, 1983), 7–8.

55. Friedman, *Capitalism and Freedom*, 45.

56. G. Epstein, interview, *Austrian Economics Newsletter*, 20 (2): 8.

57. Gage and Kearns, http://www.bloomberg.com (October 2, 2012); Bonner, http://www.dailyreckoning.com (August 11, 2012); also see Chairman Ben Bernanke's *Washington Post* Op Ed, (November 4, 2010).

58. Keynes, *General Theory*, 351.

59. John Maynard Keynes, Memo related to Macmillan Committee Report, in *Collected Writings*, vol. 20, *Activities 1929–31: Rethinking Employment and Unemployment Policies* (London: Macmillan; New York: St. Martin's Press, 1981), 273.

60. *Barron's* (September 22, 2008).

61. *Grant's Interest Rate Observer* (March 6, 2009): 7.

62. *Harvard Magazine* (November–December, 2008): 60.

63. Mises, *Human Action*, 572.

64. Hazlitt, *Failure of the "New Economics,"* 329, 331.

65. Keynes, *General Theory*, 322.

66. CNN interview, cited in *Weekly Standard* (February 2, 2009): 15; and interview with Cal Thomas, *Washington Times* (January 12, 2009), n. p.

67. Ned Davis Research, "Institutional Hotline," (June 10, 2008), 1.

68. George Akerlof and Robert Shiller, *Animal Spirits* (Princeton, NJ: Princeton University Press, 2009); see also Benjamin Friedman for a review of Akerlof and Shiller, *New York Review* (May 28, 2009): 44. In his review, Friedman notes that he made a similar proposal in "Monetary Policy with a Credit Aggregate Target," *Journal of Monetary Economics* (Spring 1983 Supplement).

69. Marc Faber, *Gloom, Boom, and Doom Report* (March 2009): 4.

70. Jean-Baptiste Say, *A Treatise on Political Economy*, 345–46; also in Randall G. Holcombe, *15 Great Austrian Economists* (Auburn, AL: Ludwig von Mises Institute, 1999), 53.

71. Paul Volcker, "Changing Fortunes," quoted in *Washington Post* (August 30, 1992): H4.

72. *Forbes* (June 19, 1995): 64.

73. Llewellyn Rockwell, *Free Market* (October 2003): 6.

74. Richard Cobden, in Frank W. Fetter, *Development of British Monetary Orthodoxy: 1797–1875* (Cambridge, MA: Harvard University Press, 1965), 176; cited in Murray N. Rothbard, *The Logic of Action II: Applications and Criticism from the Austrian School* (Lyme, NH: Edward Elgar, 1997), 323.

75. Röpke, *Free Society*, 219; also in Lewis, *Are the Rich Necessary?*, 76.

76. Friedrich A. Hayek, quoted in Sanford Ikeda, *Dynamics of the Mixed Economy: Toward a Theory of Interventionism* (London: Routledge, 1997), 183.

77. *Economist* (March 21, 2009): 83.

78. Friedrich A. Hayek, *Monetary Theory and the Trade Cycle* (London: Jonathan Cape, 1933), 21–22.

79. Ibid., 18.

80. Ibid., 19–20.

81. *Washington Times* (September 17, 2012): 34.

82. Paul Johnson, *Modern Times: The World from the Twenties to the Eighties* (New York: Harper & Row, 1983), 229.

83. *Forbes* (September 10, 2012): 14.

84. Shostak, http://www.mises.org (October 18, 2012).

85. *Weekly Standard* (February 16, 2009): 9; also *Washington Times* (March 9, 2009): 4.

86. Keynes, speech, Munich, Germany, January 8, 1932, in *Collected Writings* (vol. 21), 40, 41, 45.

87. Franco Modigliani, "Liquidity, Preference, and the Theory of Interests, and Money," *Econometrica* (January 1944): 45-88; see also Hunter Lewis, *Where Keynes Went Wrong: And Why World Governments Keep Creating Inflation, Bubbles, and Busts* (Mt. Jackson, VA: Axios Press, 2009): 219–221.

88. Paul Krugman, *Peddling Prosperity* (New York: W. W. Norton, 1994), 32; also cited in Lewis, *Are the Rich Necessary?*, 77.

89. J. Bradford DeLong and Lawrence H. Summers, Brookings Institution, *Fiscal Policy in a Depressed Economy* (March 20, 2012), cited on http://www.againstcronycapitalism.org (June 6, 2012).

90. Keynes, *General Theory*, 127.

91. Keynes, letter to Norman, (May 22, 1930), in *Collected Writings* (vol. 20), 350–56; cited in Skidelsy, *John Maynard Keynes* (vol. 2), 351.

92. *Bloomberg News* (April 15, 2009).

93. Ibid., (April 2, 2009).

94. Brannon and Batkins, http://www.washingtontimes.com (October 20, 2011).

95. Geoghegan, http://www.bloomberg.com (August 23, 2012).

96. Shiller, http://www.tnr.com (August 29, 2011).

97. Paul Krugman, *New York Times* (November 13, 2009): Opinion Page.

98. Lewis, *Where Keynes Went Wrong*, 232.

99. Keynes, *General Theory*, 264, 267.

100. http://www.marketwatch.com (August 16, 2010).

101. Johnson, *Modern Times*, 229.

102. See Chairman Ben Bernanke's *Washington Post* Op Ed (November 4, 2010).

103. Bernanke's Obfuscation, http://www.economonitor.com, a Roubini Global Economics Project (December 9, 2011).

104. *Bloomberg News* (July 20, 2009), detailing report of Neil Barofsky, special inspector general of Federal TARP (Troubled Asset Relief Program) designed to rescue banks and other financial institutions.

105. http://www.bloomberg.com (January 25, 2013).

106. Williams, http://www.shadowstats.com (December 20, 2012).

107. Krauthammer, http://www.washingtonpost.com (November 22, 2012).

108. John Goodman, http://www.healthblog.ncpa.org (July 11, 2012).

109. Lawrence Kotlikoff, http://www.bloomberg.com (August 8, 2012).

110. Gehrke, http://www.washingtonexaminer.com (January 14, 2013).

111. Keynes, *General Theory*, 327, 322, 320–22.

112. *New York Times* (August 2, 2002).

113. Ibid., (October 30, 2006).

114. *Economist* (December 6, 2008): 94.
115. Robert Solow, *New York Review of Books* (May 14, 2009): 6.
116. *The New Yorker* (September 21, 2009): 60.
117. *Economist* (October 14, 2010).
118. CNN interview, cited in *Weekly Standard* (February 2, 2009): 15; and interview with Cal Thomas, *Washington Times* (January 12, 2009), n.p.
119. *Grant's Interest Rate Observer* (November 4, 2011): 1.
120. *Bloomberg Business Week* (August 17, 2010).
121. *New York Times* (January 19, 2010).
122. *Grant's Interest Rate Observer* (December 16, 2011): 6.
123. *Grant's Interest Rate Observer* (October 21, 2011): 11 and *Washington Times* (July 25, 2011): 38.
124. BBC radio interview (December 21, 2012).
125. *Grant's Interest Rate Observer* (November 4, 2011): 1.
126. *Washington Post* (April 13, 2012).
127. *Wall Street Journal* (June 24, 2008).
128. Barclay's estimate cited in *Economist*, (October 17, 2009): 84.
129. Rothbard, *Case Against the Fed*, 42.
130. Caroline Baum, *Bloomberg View* (May 23, 2012).
131. *Newsweek* (June 22, 2009): 42.
132. *Hussman Letter* (September 28, 2009): 1.
133. Paul McCulley, *PIMCO Letter* (November 13, 2008):7.
134. *Grant's Interest Rate Observer* (July 27, 2012): 10.
135. Guido Hülsmann, *The Ethics of Money Production* (Auburn, AL: Ludwig von Mises Institute, 2008); see also Lewis, *Are the Rich Necessary?*, 321–38.
136. Rockwell, *Free Market* (February 2009): 3–4.
137. Dr. Ron Paul address to Congress (August 13, 2012).

138. *Grant's Interest Rate Observer* (July 24, 2009): 3.

139. Alexander Hamilton, Report to the House of Representatives, December 13, 1790, in American State Papers, Finance, 1st Congress, 3rd Session, no. 18, I, 67–76; also quoted in Jude Wanniski, *The Way the World Works: How Economies Fail—and Succeed* (New York: Basic Books, 1978), 204–5.

140. Wanniski, *The Way the World Works*, 205.

141. Andrew Jackson, Farewell Address, March 4, 1837; also in George Seldes, *Great Thoughts* (New York: Ballantine, 1985), 202.

142. http://www.mises.org/daily/6141/ (August 23, 2012).

143. Keynes, *General Theory*, 164. Also John Maynard Keynes, *Collected Writings*, vol 6, *A Treatise on Money: The Applied Theory of Money* (London: Macmillan; New York: St. Martin's Press, 1971), 145.

144. Keynes, BBC Broadcast, *Collected Writings*, (vol 21), 86.

145. Keynes, BBC Broadcast, *Collected Writings*, (vol 20), 325.

146. *Weekly Standard* (January 19, 2009): 20.

147. Skidelsky, *John Maynard Keynes* (vol. 2), 224.

148 Keynes, *Collected Writings*, (vol. 20), 515.

149. Keynes, *Collected Writings*, vol. 4, *Tract on Monetary Reform* (London: Macmillan; New York: St. Martin's Press, 1971), 159; (vol. 6), 268, 303.

150. Robert Heilbroner, *New Yorker* (January 23, 1989); also in Michael Novak, *Spirit of Democratic Capitalism* (New York: Madison Books, 1982), 417–18.

151. *Economist* (September 20, 1997): 5.

152. Brink Lindsey, *Against the Dead Hand: The Uncertain Struggle for Global Capitalism* (New York: John Wiley & Sons, 2002), xi.

153. James Grant, interview, *Austrian Economics Newsletter*, 16, no 4 (Winter 1996): 2–3.

154. William Anderson, *Free Market* (June 2003): 6.

155. Ned Davis Research, *Chart of the Day*, (February 22, 2005): 1 and (May 10, 2005): 1.

156. *Grant's Interest Rate Observer* (October 5, 2012): 1.

157. Marc Faber, *Gloom, Boom, and Doom Report* (January 2013): 3.

158. *Washington Times*, (June 25, 2012): 29.

159. "The Bank Credit Analyst," *The Outlook* (January 1996): 30.

160. *Bloomberg News* (July 24, 2009).

161. John P. Hussman, *Weekly Market Comment* (December 17, 2012).

162. http://www.economonitor.com (August 11, 2012).

163. Ronald McKinnon, *Wall Street Journal* (September 30, 2011): A-15.

164. Lenzner, http://www.forbes.com (June 3, 2010).

165. Ibid.

166. Censky, http://www.money.cnn.com (March 26, 2012).

167. Friedman, *Free to Choose*, 81.

168. Marc Faber, *Tomorrow's Gold: Asia's Age of Discovery* (Hong Kong: CLSA, 2002), 346–47.

169. Keynes, *General Theory*, 235.

170. Paul Kasriel, *Northern Trust Economic Research* (March 30, 2001).

171. Lewis, *Are the Rich Necessary?*, 175–77.

172. *The Commercial and Financial Chronicle* (November 21, 1957), quoted in James Grant, *The Trouble with Prosperity: The Loss of Fear, the Rise of Speculation, and the Risk to American Savings* (New York: Random House, 1996), 37–38; also in Hunter Lewis, *How Much Money Does An Economy Need?: Solving the Central Economic Puzzle of Money, Prices, and Jobs* (Mt. Jackson, VA: Axios Press, 2007), 19.

173. John Maynard Keynes, *Collected Writings,* vol. 10, *Essays in Biography* (London: Macmillan; New York: St. Martin's Press, 1972), 446–47, second note.

174. O'Driscoll, http://www.onlinewsj.com (April 20, 2010).

175. Malpass, *Forbes* (December 20, 2012).

176. Pollack, http://www.aei-ideas-org (November 18, 2011).

177. http://www.bloomberg.com (September 28, 2011).

178. Firm client letters, November 22, 2010 and December 13, 2010 among others.

179. Durden, http://www.zerohedge.com (December 6, 2012).

180. 1999 speech "Japanese Monetary Policy – A Case of Self-Induced Paralysis?"

181. Dr. Ron Paul before the House of Representatives, December 13, 2010.

182. Ivry, http://www.bloomberg.com (May 26, 2011).

183. Dr. Ron Paul before the House of Representatives, April 18, 2011.

184. De Carbonnel, http://www.marketskeptics.com (March 29, 2009).

185. Toune, http://www.touneforcongress.com (June and September 8, 2009).

186. Quoted in Faber, http://www.alternet.org and *Gloom, Boom and Doom Report* (October 2012): 4.

187. *Business Week* (May 20, 1985): 38.

188. *Grant's Interest Rate Observer* (April 20, 2012): 5.

189. Barone, http://www.washingtonexaminer.com (December 4, 2012); also Federal tax receipts as percent of GDP http://www.wikipedia.org.

190. Will, http://www.washingtonpost.com (January 5, 2012).

191. Paul Johnson, *History of Christianity* (New York: Simon and Schuster, 1976), Part 5.

192. *The Economist* (March 20, 2010): 91.

193. Caplan, http://www.econlong.econlib.org (March 4, 2010).

194. http://www.wsj.com (October 1, 2011).

195. Rich Miller, *Bloomberg News* (May 19, 2009).

196. Akerlof and Shiller, *Animal Spirits*; see also Benjamin Friedman for a review of Akerlof and Shiller, *New York Review* (May 28, 2009): 44. In his review, Friedman notes that he made a similar proposal in "Monetary Policy with a Credit Aggregate Target," *Journal of Monetary Economics* (Spring 1983 Supplement).

197. http://www.againstcronycapitalism.org (November 28, 2011).

198. *Forbes* (July 16, 2012): 24.

199. Lawrence Kotlikoff, http://www.bloomberg.com (September 28, 2011).

200. Ken Mayland, http://www.marketwatch.com (August 16, 2010).

201. Ayres and Edlin, *New York Times* (December 19, 2011): A-29.

202. Quoted in *Grant's Interest Rate Observer* (June 15, 2012): 5.

203. William Pesek, http://www.bloomberg.com (May 21, 2012).

204. http://www.againstcronycapitalism.org (June 8, 2012).

205. Jim Rogers, Investment Biker, quoted on Roger's blog, accessed November 8, 2012.

206. House Ways and Means Committee, May 1939, quoted in Burton Folsom, *New Deal or Raw Deal? How FDR's Economic Legacy Has Damaged America*

(New York: Threshold Editions, 2008); quoted Charen, http://www.nationalreview.com (November 25, 2012).

207. Walter Lippmann, *The Good Society* (Boston: Little Brown, 1943), 119.

208. Conroy, http://www.realclearpolitics.com (December 6, 2012).

209. http://www.againstcronycapitalism.org (January 9, 2012).

210. Ibid. (July 16, 2012).

211. Thomas Sowell, http://www.townhall.com (December 12, 2012).

212. Alan Blinder, *Hard Heads, Soft Hearts: Tough-Minded Economics for a Just Society* (Cambridge, MA: Perseus Books, 1987); quoted in Samuelson, *Washington Post* (September 7, 1994): A21.

213. *Forbes* (August 6, 2001): 77.

214. Faber, *Gloom, Boom, and Doom Report* (May 14, 2011), 10.

215. Ned Davis commentary (May 28, 2009).

216. McDonald, http://www.foxbusiness.com (December 13, 2012).

217. Faber, *Gloom, Boom, and Doom Report.*

218. *Forbes* (October 22, 2012): 19.

219. Tamny, http://www.realclearmarkets.com (December 6, 2012).

220. Letter to John Tyler, 1816.

221. President Jackson's veto message regarding the Bank of the United States: (July 10, 1832), http://www.avalon.law.yale.edu.

222. John Hobson, *Richard Cobden: The International Man* (London: 1919), 392.

223. *Grant's Interest Rate Observer* (July 13, 2012): 1.

224. Pipes, http://www.forbes.com (August 20, 2012).

225. Smith, http://www.nypost.com (October 2, 2010).

226. Lester Brown press release, November 6, 2001.

227. William Hutt, *The Theory of Idle Resources* (London: Jonathan Cape, 1939), 18.

228. Keynes, *General Theory*, n.p.

229. Lippman, *The Good Society*, 193–94; also in Novak, *Spirit of Democratic Capitalism*, 100.

230. http://www.wsj.com (October 12, 2012).

Index

B